London Writing

London Writing

Merlin Coverley

www.pocketessentials.com

This edition published in 2005 by Pocket Essentials
P.O.Box 394, Harpenden, Herts, AL5 1XJ

Distributed in the USA by Trafalgar Square Publishing, P.O. Box 257, Howe Hill
Road, North Pomfret, Vermont 05053
http:// www.pocketessentials.com

A CIP catalogue record for this book is available from the British Library.

ISBN 1 904048 48 X

2 4 6 8 10 9 7 5 3 1

Typeset by Avocet Typeset, Chilton, Aylesbury, Bucks
Printed and bound in Great Britain by Cox & Wyman, Reading, Berks

Acknowledgements

My thanks to Chris Sykes for providing the initial momentum for this project, Ion Mills for his advice and enthusiasm, and Catherine for her support throughout.

Contents

CONTENTS

Introduction

'In this city everything connects.'
Peter Ackroyd, *London: The Biography* (2000)

Where to begin? If there is one point on which London writers appear to agree, it is the fact that London is endless, illimitable, a world too huge and complex to be accurately captured by a single author, let alone a single text. Yet not only is the city regarded as an unknowable labyrinth, it is also eternal, defying chronological order through an endless cycle of decline and regeneration. If this is true of the city, then it is equally true of the writing it has inspired. Iain Sinclair has described the growth of London writing as similar to a viral culture, one writer both leading back toward his predecessors and anticipating those who are to follow; each text an accumulation of the past and a prediction for the future together creating new genres and traditions and branching off in new and unexpected directions. In a city where everything connects, where does one begin?

The writers that I wish to include here all treat London as something more than a mere backdrop. In these works, London becomes a character in its own right, whose presence is bound together with the lives that are lived within its fictional borders. Of course, in the absence of a rigorous definition of what constitutes London writing (as opposed to that which is simply writing about London), there must inevitably be a largely arbitrary and subjective nature to one's choices, while others become necessary due to the limitations of this project. It is difficult to imagine a pocket that could find room for an overview of London writing in its entirety and so boundaries must be drawn. The most obvious way of achieving this seems to be to decide upon the type of writing to be included. The strongest and most clearly sustained tradition of London writing and the one that is most widely represented today is that of the novel. Poetry and plays, biography and history, essays and journalism all have had, and continue to have, a strong claim upon the history of London writing, but it is to the novel that I will confine myself in this book. Of course, this means that at a stroke some of the greatest names in London, and indeed world, literature are omitted, amongst them Chaucer and Shakespeare, Samuel Pepys and Dr Johnson, Spenser and Blake, De Quincey and Charles Lamb. Furthermore, not only am I choosing the most representative London novelists, but I am also choosing their most representative London novels and each writer will be confined here to a single entry. In this way, I will be able to draw up a shortlist of the 30 essential London novels.

In his book, *The Soul of London* (1905), Ford Madox Ford famously observed:

'England is a small island
The world is infinitesimal
But London is illimitable.'

And writing almost a century later Peter Ackroyd echoed these comments:

'London goes beyond any boundary or convention. It contains every wish or word ever spoken, every action or gesture ever made, every harsh or noble statement ever expressed. It is illimitable. It is infinite London.'

Now, having chosen the novel as the most representative strand of London writing, it is necessary to decide which writers and which novels most closely reflect these sentiments.

If the starting point of the novel is taken to be the early eighteenth century, there are few obvious candidates who describe the city with a sufficient sense of place to be identified as having written the first London novel. Daniel Defoe in *Moll Flanders* (1722) and later *Roxana* (1724) records with great relish both London's lowlife and the opulence of the King's Court, but his most memorable account of London is that of the plague years of his youth in *A Journal of the Plague Year* (1722), which, while certainly in large part a work of fiction, was at least presented as a work of fact.

Henry Fielding and Tobias Smollett were both novelists whose work might be considered a suitable starting point for the London novel. Fielding's *Jonathan*

Wild (1743) offers a fictional account of one of the most famous Londoners of his day. Similarly, *Tom Jones* (1749) also deals with the underworld of Georgian London, contrasting urban scenes of vice and degradation with the honest simplicity of the rural existence beyond the city's boundaries. Both novels provide significant descriptions of the London of that era, but here the city is never more than a part of a wider canvas and these are primarily morality plays in which London symbolises only one part of human behaviour, the seedier part, without the totalising sense of a self-contained world that is the hallmark of the true London novelist. In a similar vein, Smollett's picaresque London adventures continue a fascination with London's squalid underbelly that has rarely diminished since. But once again, neither *The Adventures of Roderick Random* (1748) nor *The Expedition of Humphrey Clinker* (1771) really reflect the stature of London as a world-city. To be fair, it is perhaps less a question of the stature of these novels than the stature of the city they are describing, for London in its Georgian incarnation was still a long way from attaining the unimaginable magnitude and complexity that was to define the Victorian megalopolis. If we are looking for a fictional representation that equates London with the world, then we must fast-forward to the nineteenth century and the birth of the city that remains in many respects the one we inhabit today.

Once in the Victorian era, we can breathe a sigh of relief and immediately give up the pretence that anyone other than Charles Dickens is the man to begin a survey of the London novel. So huge and influential are his portrayals of London that one could easily devote this entire survey to his novels alone. Needless to say, once his name has been introduced, the novelists that precede him become little more than precursors who, while influential, seem rather lightweight by comparison. For just as Shakespeare is often said to have invented the English language, so Dickens appears to have not so much described London as to have invented our conception of it and it is to this source that almost all subsequent London fiction is indebted.

Having found a starting point, it is now necessary to devise a principle by which order can be brought to the chaotic mass of authors and novels that have since placed London at the heart of their work. At first, it is tempting to see London's history and its parallel history in the novel as a straightforward narrative unfolding in a linear progression, but time in London appears to be governed by its own laws, operating at different speeds in different quarters of the city, seeming to progress only to relapse back to an earlier stage. In this way, events are repeated and different histories replayed as time moves in a circular fashion. In his mammoth biography of the city Peter Ackroyd notes:

'There are many forms of time in the city, and it would be foolish of me to change its character for the sake of erecting a conventional narrative. That is why this book moves quixotically through time, itself forming a labyrinth. If the history of London poverty is beside a history of London madness, then the

connections may provide more significant information than any historiographical survey.'

This conception of time will be my guiding principle
too and accordingly this survey will be structured less
by chronology than by theme.

If, then, time in London is seen as cyclical, so too is
the fictional tradition that seeks to reflect it. In this
manner, writers who are fêted by one generation may
subsequently disappear without trace, often to reappear
once again at a later stage. Thus while Dickens may
now shape our perception of the Victorian city, it was
his contemporary GWM Reynolds who commanded
the greater readership in the early part of Victoria's
reign. Yet who can honestly claim to have heard of, let
alone read, his melodramatic novel *The Mysteries of
London* (1845). Similarly, while William Pett Ridge was
amongst the most famous literary Londoners of his day
and remains vigorously championed by writers such as
Michael Moorcock, his London novels have long since
been consigned to oblivion. I shall be devoting a
chapter of this survey to lost London writers whose
works have, in my opinion, been unjustly neglected. Yet
many writers require no such resurrection, their works
apparently transcending the cyclical current that has
submerged so many of their contemporaries. These
figures are the giants of London writing, whose works
now form the established canon and who created not
only new characters and visions of the city, but in some
cases inaugurated entirely new genres.

Dickens' heavyweight contenders include both

William Thackeray and Anthony Trollope, but neither can be regarded as true London writers. For while Dickens' imaginative universe is largely circumscribed by the city, Thackeray's *Vanity Fair* (1847) treats London only as an oblique part of a larger whole and Trollope's Palliser novels, whilst creating memorable observations of London's political elites, remain less clearly realised than his rural Barsetshire. Elsewhere, however, the true inheritance of Dickens' London gradually emerges, as the bleak realism of London poverty is given voice in a range of novels, from Arthur Morrison's *Tales of the Mean Streets* (1894) and *A Child of the Jago* (1896) to Israel Zangwill's *Children of the Ghetto* (1892), so raising awareness of the squalid plight of many Londoners. Meanwhile, the comic tradition is extended through George and Weedon Grossmith's *Diary of a Nobody* (1892) and Jerome K Jerome's Thames-side excursion *Three Men in a Boat* (1889) and on through GK Chesterton's whimsical tale of a future London, *The Napoleon of Notting Hill* (1892).

Images of future Londons are widespread in the novels of the late nineteenth century and find their most utopian expression in *News From Nowhere* (1891) by William Morris, in which we are offered a curious blend of socialist and pastoral idyll as blushing maidens and strapping young men furiously weave and thatch their way to an egalitarian paradise. Such a vision of London's future is, of course, a return to London's pre-industrial past and taps into early anxieties regarding the dangers of industrialisation. In a similar vein Richard Jefferies' *After London* (1885) describes a city that literally drowns in its own effluent, but he is more ambivalent about the merits of a return to the land. Such prophetic novels generally combine a political critique of London present alongside a steadfast belief in a brighter future, but in combining such hopes and fears with an awareness of the potential of technological progress, HG Wells ushered in the new genre of science fiction. Wells was to write extensively about London in a realist mode, both in *Anna Veronica* (1909) and *Tono-Bungay* (1909), in which he explores the claustrophobia of Edwardian class structures and anxieties over the huge expansion in London's population alongside controversial issues of sex, marriage and independence. Yet it is in his earlier 'scientific romances' that his enduring appeal lies and where we find the finest examples of his use of London as a setting. In *The Invisible Man* (1897) the newly invisible narrator tries to negotiate a familiarly overcrowded Oxford Street, while in *The War of the Worlds* (1898) we can once again enjoy the peculiar pleasure of witnessing London's violent destruction. This book is an early example of the disaster novel that was later to reappear with renewed force in novels such as John Wyndham's *The Day of the Triffids* (1951) and JG Ballard's *The Drowned World* (1962).

Wells' most enduring legacy to the London novel, however, is a work that has very little overt connection with the city. *The Time Machine* (1895) takes the stark inequalities of Victorian London to their logical conclusion by portraying a distant future in which the indolent Eloi are both served and consumed by their bestial underground cousins, the Morlocks, and the idea of an environment in which surface normality is undercut by an underground city in parallel with it finds great currency in recent London writing. Contemporary examples such as Christopher Fowler's *Roofworld* (1988), Neil Gaiman's *Neverwhere* (1997) and Conrad Williams' *London Revenant* (2004) all explore Londons behind, below and above the city of our everyday experience.

Science fiction is not the only new genre to emerge during this period, for through such novels as Wilkie Collins' *The Moonstone* (1868) the detective novel was to gain enormous and enduring popularity and remains especially important to London writing. It has been argued that the detective genre is particularly suited to London and its labyrinthine streets through the requirement of the plot for specific and recognisable coordinates for the set pieces, yet it seems to me that in much of London's finest detective fiction, London becomes not only the setting but a part of the mystery itself. Nowhere is this more true than in the works of Sir Arthur Conan Doyle, whose creation Sherlock Holmes is so powerfully equated with the mythic London of swirling fog and hansom cabs that he is single-handedly responsible for much of the disappointment today's tourists feel on encountering a city so conspicuously lacking in penny-farthings and deerstalkers. In novels such as *A Study in Scarlet* (1887) and *The Sign of Four* (1890), in addition to the numerous short stories, London is as much a puzzle as the crime itself; a maze that must be unravelled, and knowledge of the layout of the city is crucial to Holmes' success.

A subtle mutation of the detective novel gave rise to the spy novel, and while Erskine Childers' *The Riddle of the Sands* (1903) leads the way, Joseph Conrad's magnificent *The Secret Agent* (1907), based on a real life Anarchist 'outrage' in Greenwich Park, offers a truly prescient image of the hypocrisy and twisted motives behind terrorism and lays bare the reality of a profession that was soon to acquire a veneer of exotic attraction for later practitioners of the genre.

So, now we can begin to chart the emergence of those themes that have dominated London fiction since its inception – here we have both the acknowledged heavyweights of the canon, as well as its less celebrated exponents. There is both comedy and fantasy alongside the harsh realities of urban life. The utopian vision is contrasted with apocalyptic renderings of future London and, along with science fiction, we find the worlds of the criminal and the spy. Finally, there is that strand of London writing that is perhaps most clearly associated with the London of the late nineteenth century and is once again so widely appropriated today – the occult.

The canonical text here is Robert Louis Stevenson's *The Strange Case of Dr Jekyll and Mr Hyde* (1886). Originally published as a 'shilling shocker', this novel made Stevenson's reputation and was enormously influential upon other practitioners of the London Occult, such as Oscar Wilde and Arthur Machen. Here, the central idea of the split personality is projected onto the fogbound London streets, and in recalling the horrible fascination of Dickens' portrayals of the London slums, Stevenson succeeds in transforming London into a reflection of the psychological states he is describing. In this, he has rightly been described by the critic Robert Mighall as London's first psychogeographer, portraying London in cinematic, even mythical, terms. Indeed, the fictional world of Mr Hyde was soon to find factual support in the figure of Jack the Ripper, fusing the London of fiction and reality in such a powerful way that the London of this time has effectively foreshadowed everything that was to follow. As a consequence, the London fictions of the twenties and thirties in many ways describe a city still recognisably the same and right up until the outbreak of the Second World War, London writing continues to resonate with images of poorly lit streets and yellow fog obscuring shady characters.

As fog gave way to smog, so occult themes gradually subsided as the 'golden era' of the crime novel arrived. Both Gerald Kersh's *Night and the City* (1938) and later Margery Allingham's *The Tiger in the Smoke* (1952) were to become films and both, with varying degrees of success, attempt to map the familiar routes of lowlife London, while the now totally forgotten works of James Curtis and Robert Westerby ensured that fictional crimes remained resolutely small time in their tales of failure and revenge in the boozers of pre-war London.

If much of the London writing between the wars is characterised by an obscurity in both its subject matter of invisible lives, as well as in the fate of these authors and their books, this period also produced markedly more memorable, or at least more widely remembered, fictions from a parallel London of picnics and blazers. For while small-time crooks were dreaming of a big heist, the 1920s and 1930s were, for the fictional characters celebrated by, amongst others, Evelyn Waugh, Aldous Huxley, Wyndham Lewis and Virginia Woolf, decades of seemingly unbroken leisure. Novels such as *Mrs Dalloway* (1925) and *Point Counter Point* (1928), *Vile Bodies* (1930) and *The Apes of God* (1930) recount, often in excruciating detail, the lives or sometimes simply the days of a small coterie of characters with artistic pretensions who wander between Bloomsbury and Mayfair on their way to a seemingly endless round of dinner parties.

In retrospect, the Second World War merely highlights the fragility of upper-class life in the London of this period, and certainly in post-war fiction the gulf between these two Londons of spivs and toffs is much less broad. The war may have continued class distinctions through the opposing ranks of officers and men, yet it also appears to have drawn together the more disparate strands of London fiction by producing its own easily recognisable sense of wartime dislocation. From Patrick Hamilton's celebrated *Hangover Square* (1941) to Norman Collins' less well-known *London Belongs to Me* (1945), the familiar London of pubs and boarding houses takes on a new sense of anxiety and unease in the face of the impending war. Elsewhere, Graham Greene's *The Ministry of Fear* (1943) and Elizabeth Bowen's *The Heat of the Day* (1945) explore the reality of the Blitz, during which life and relationships are overtaken by an eerie sense of disorientation as the familiar landscape of the city is reduced to rubble. Henry Green most vividly portrays this sense of heightened unreality in his novel *Caught* (1943), in which an account of the Blitz from the perspective of the London firefighters, of whom Green was a member, is surprisingly underscored by an increasingly bizarre account of the relationships between them. Soon a novel that one might expect to provide a conventional wartime account of heroism and camaraderie gives way to a much less wholesome subplot of sexual intrigue and mental imbalance.

If, then, the war is to be taken as a definitive break with the past, both culturally and politically, it follows that such a break should be apparent within the tradition of London writing. For some writers, however, the war had only a minor impact and they remained largely oblivious to it as they sat marooned in the pubs of Soho and Fitzrovia. The most representative writer of this group is Julian Maclaren-Ross, whose limited artistic output was a result of a protracted bout of 'Sohoitis', the inability to translate increasingly grandiose plans into any kind of material reality. Maclaren-Ross, whose memoirs were unsurprisingly difficult to recollect and remained unfinished at the time of his death, did, however, manage to produce a quantity of short stories whose London settings have recently found a new audience.

While writers such as Maclaren-Ross and the Fitzrovia set continued through the war years in much the same vein as before, much post-war writing about

London returns to recreate these years in its fiction. Graham Greene's *The End of the Affair* (1951) for example, is largely biographical, revisiting the Blitz and the house off Clapham Common where he once lived. But the 1950s are not entirely a period of nostalgic recollection, and while the shortages and austerity remained a constant reminder of the war, some writers such as Colin MacInnes were able to detect the youthful unrest that was to explode in the following decade. His London trilogy, *City of Spades* (1957), *Absolute Beginners* (1959) and *Mr Love and Justice* (1960), portray the early bohemian lifestyles of West London and are also notable for their reflection of the effects of post-war immigration and the tensions that culminated in the Notting Hill race riots of 1958. But this era finds its most authentic voice in Sam Selvon's *The Lonely Londoners* (1956), in which Selvon, himself a West Indian immigrant, uses the Trinidadian dialect to accurately recreate the conflicting sense of excitement and apprehension felt by many on arriving in London for the first time.

A few years later in Alexander Baron's *The Lowlife* (1961), we are once again returned to the gambling, petty crime and cramped boarding houses that seem an eternal staple of London fiction. Baron provides access to a particularly fertile strand of Jewish London writing, which includes figures such as Bernard Kops and Emmanuel Litvinoff whose autobiographical *Journey Through a Small Planet* (1972) vividly recalls the sights and smells of a Jewish East End that was soon to vanish forever.

The 1950s, however, are equally memorable for the re-emergence of a quite different mode of London writing, that of the disaster novel. Following in the footsteps of Jefferies and Wells, the novels of John Wyndham and John Christopher, and later Christopher Priest and M John Harrison, all recount a variety of catastrophic scenarios. Yet out of what is essentially a British subgenre of quite conventional and conservative sympathies, JG Ballard's early disaster novels have introduced some of the most experimental and disturbing images of the modern city. His first, and by his own admission largely forgettable, novel, *The Wind from Nowhere* (1962), depicts London at the mercy of increasing winds, and shortly afterwards *The Drowned World* (1962) was once again to describe a London of the near future. This time the catastrophe is flood, as rising temperatures return London to the state of a primordial swamp, albeit a rather comfortable one with the protagonist ensconced in a penthouse at the Ritz. This later novel is a far more accomplished attempt to portray a post-apocalyptic city, but it was criticised by many as continuing the convention of the 'cosy catastrophe', in which the future demise of the city allows the survivors to live a strangely glamorous lifestyle. In this sense, Ballard's novel fulfils this criterion for comfort, but also proceeds to undermine our expectations as the protagonist gradually succumbs to the charms of the drowned city and ultimately wanders off into the jungle in a mood of dream-like passivity.

Ballard's novels of the 1960s and 70s combine both a

radical experimentalism with a cautionary note to those inspired by an unwavering belief in the potential of technological change. *Crash* (1973) *Concrete Island* (1974) and *High-Rise* (1975) form a loose trilogy of novels exploring the newly developing world of motorways, airports and supermarkets, a neon-lit non-place of suburban anonymity that barely qualifies as London writing, describing as it does that marginal zone where the city loses its identity, becoming that familiar yet indistinguishable space that seems to encircle all modern urban centres. Ballard explores the bizarre and unexpected behaviour such a landscape may provoke, and in his preference for the suburbs he follows a trajectory away from the historical centre of the city that has been extremely influential on other London writers, such as Iain Sinclair and Chris Petit.

Meanwhile, the largely unheralded novels of Maureen Duffy continue to explore peripheral communities within London and her London 'triptych', *Wounds* (1969), *Capital* (1975) and *Londoners* (1983), both anticipates the radical changes wrought by Thatcherism, as well as dramatising London's history in a manner that has become much more fashionable today. Another writer operating in the 1960s and 70s who explored the marginal places and lives of the city was Robin Cook (later to become Derek Raymond), a crime novelist of the darkest and bleakest variety who depicts a city of windblown refuse and decay populated by the lonely, vulnerable and violent. Early satires such as *The Tenants of Dirt Street* (1971) were followed by a switch to the crime novel and books such as *I Was Dora*

Suarez (1991) burn with anger at the declining fortunes of a city that is always implicated in the sordid crimes Raymond describes. Raymond was a friend of Sinclair, who in turn was an admirer and sometime collaborator of Ballard and Moorcock, and it seems that much of the London writing of this period and indeed the present day is largely a closed shop of self-promoting and self-mythologising writers engaged in a shared agenda. Sinclair's 'London Project', which describes his mixture of fiction and documentary writings on the city, combines many of the traditional themes of London fiction such as the criminal and the occult, with a powerful political critique of contemporary London. This political engagement was especially apparent throughout the Thatcherite period and challenged an ideology that resulted in the bland and unimaginative redevelopment of large swathes of the city. The key novels here are Peter Ackroyd's *Hawksmoor* (1985), a detective fiction that uses the pretext of an occult alignment between Hawksmoor's six remaining London churches to establish a vision of 1980s London through the eyes of its emerging underclass. This novel was largely inspired by Iain Sinclair's *Lud Heat* (1975), a prose poem which first expounded this occult theory, and Sinclair's London novels such as *White Chappell Scarlet Tracings* (1987) and *Downriver* (1991) use an occult content to expose and satirise the profound effects of Thatcherite policies on the fabric of the city. In a similar vein but with a historical sweep encompassing the city from the time of the Blitz to the 1980s, Michael Moorcock's *Mother London* (1988) has been described as a love letter to a city now largely forgotten. This epic novel is filled with the voices of earlier Londoners whose stories still resonate through the streets.

This interweaving of historical detail, political protest and occult significance forms the hallmark of much contemporary London fiction, and writers as diverse as Chris Petit in *Robinson* (1993), Geoff Nicholson in *Bleeding London* (1997) and Stewart Home in his ultra-violent parody *Red London* (1994) continue to produce off-beat accounts of a largely overlooked city. Of course, these writers themselves have in many instances gone unnoticed, but in other genres London writing continues to flourish. In crime writers such as Mark Timlin and Anthony Frewin we have natural successors to Derek Raymond's London *noir*, whilst Christopher Fowler, Neil Gaiman and Alan Moore reflect the revival of interest in Gothic representations of the city and a return to the occult preoccupations of the late nineteenth century.

While the novels and authors outlined above will always remain a largely subjective and sometimes idiosyncratic selection from a potentially limitless source of London writing, it will become clear in the following selection of the 30 essential London novels that in large part I have purposely favoured the obscure over the celebrated and the marginal over the mainstream. Thus while Martin Amis' *London Fields* (1989) appears impossible to ignore regardless of its faults, other recent and similarly popular London novels such as Zadie Smith's *White Teeth* (2000) and Monica Ali's *Brick Lane*

(2003) have not been included in this account. For despite these London-orientated titles, I immediately felt a sense of resistance to their inclusion in a survey such as this. The reasons for this resistance are difficult to articulate clearly, but there remains a sense that these hugely successful and greatly acclaimed novels conform less to a tradition of London writing that celebrates the hidden and obscure than to a 'brand' of London writing, a marketed image of the city too heavily sponsored by a sense of what London ought to be rather than what it has actually become. Of course, notions of what is 'real' London and what is not can never be satisfactorily resolved and in the end one is always forced back upon questions of personal taste. But as this survey must inevitably provide a cross-section rather than a whole, it is a sample that, however inconsistent and unconventional, and however haphazard in its choices, can confidently claim to represent a city that is equally unreliable, equally disordered and by its very nature equally impossible to grasp in its entirety.

The London Canon

.

'Then the vision of an enormous town presented itself, of a monstrous town more populous than some continents and in its man-made might as if indifferent to heaven's frowns and smiles; a cruel devourer of the world's light. There was room enough there to place any story, depth enough there for any passion, variety enough there for any setting, darkness enough to bury five millions of lives.'

Joseph Conrad, Author's Note
(1920) to *The Secret Agent*

Much of this Pocket Essential is devoted to the neglected and the overlooked, to those figures and texts that occupy the margins of London's literary history, and yet residing over and in opposition to this forgotten tradition is the London Canon, the roll-call of those celebrated novels that demand inclusion within any overview of London writing. These novels act as milestones upon a literary journey that begins in the Victorian city and while I have explored the origins of the London novel in my introduction and have clearly demonstrated the primacy of Dickens' position within the London Canon, there are other novelists whose works have also endured the test of time to become classics. The novels that are included here are not incidentally about London – they are great novels precisely because of their success as great London novels. The examples I have chosen represent a brief period and are largely the product of the Victorian and Edwardian eras, and this remains a particularly fertile period for the London novel, encompassing both the naturalism of the late nineteenth century and the emerging modernism of the early twentieth.

One might certainly make a case for later London novels to be included here, but I have been reluctant to extend the London Canon to include novels whose inclusion might be premature. Penguin might feel able to reissue Martin Amis' *Money* (1984) as a modern classic less than 20 years after it was written, but such an example seems to me simply to reinforce the need for caution in ascribing classic status. Furthermore, this is a list that is to be read alongside those writers featured in the following chapters who, in pioneering other genres, might as easily have warranted inclusion here, amongst them Robert Louis Stevenson and William Morris, Sir Arthur Conan Doyle and HG Wells.

Throughout this book I have followed the principle of choosing only one novel to represent the work of one author and nowhere has this rule been more severely tested than in the case of Charles Dickens. Dickens' entire oeuvre is dominated by his portrayal of London and its inhabitants and there are several notable contenders for his greatest London novel, amongst them *Oliver Twist* (1838), *Little Dorritt* (1857), and *Our*

Mutual Friend (1865). In choosing *Bleak House* (1853), however, I have included a book that best captures the labyrinthine aspect of the city and in whose opening lines we find perhaps the greatest passage of London prose yet written.

George Gissing is as close an English writer we have to the harsh realism of Zola and his novel *New Grub Street* (1891) is in many ways the London novelist's London novel, describing both the joy and the despair, but mainly the despair, of those who have attempted to record the lives of their fellow Londoners.

Joseph Conrad, unlike many of the other figures discussed here, is by no means primarily a London writer, but his sole London novel, *The Secret Agent* (1907), is one of his finest and uses a real-life terrorist incident to inspire what is one of the earliest fictional accounts of espionage. Conrad is noticeably more modern in his approach than his predecessors, with his tale of betrayal and twisted motives anticipating the moral uncertainties of Graham Greene.

Mrs Dalloway (1925) is the high-water mark for Modernist London fiction and is certainly something of an acquired taste. Her account of a single day in the life of Clarissa Dalloway is undoubtedly a sophisticated attempt at rendering the varied sights, sounds and impressions of the city as they ebb and flow but is more likely to inspire admiration than affection in its readership.

Finally, Evelyn Waugh, like Woolf, remains firmly bound by the narrow class distinctions of his day, but *Vile Bodies* (1930) injects some much needed humour into a Canon whose prevailing mood is one of hopeless misery.

In all these novels we can recognise the emergence of new ways of apprehending the city and many of the themes that are explored later in this book are rehearsed here. For the London Canon portrays the city in its entirety from the slums of the East End to the power and privilege of the City and records the experiences of its inhabitants as they move from comedy to tragedy, from the outlandish to the everyday.

Charles Dickens, *Bleak House* (1853)

Author and Background: Charles Dickens was born in Portsmouth in 1812 and after a happy childhood in Chatham moved to London in 1823. Soon faced with financial disaster, however, Dickens began work in a blacking factory while the remainder of his family were placed in the debtors prison, an experience that was to haunt him for life.

Having received a rudimentary schooling and after a brief stint as a solicitor's clerk and parliamentary reporter, Dickens produced his first novel, *The Pickwick Papers*, in 1836–7. Published as a cheap serial publication, the success of the novel made Dickens' name and many more were to follow, including *Oliver Twist* (1838) and *Nicholas Nickleby* (1839). A period of travel in the USA and Europe ensued; by now, Dickens was a publishing phenomenon and in great demand. Writing at a prodigious rate, Dickens completed the novels on which his fame now rests, with the largely autobiographical *David Copperfield* (1850), followed by *Bleak House* (1853), *Little Dorritt* (1857) and *Great Expectations* (1861). His later years were dogged by ill health and his final novel, *The Mystery of Edwin Drood*, remained unfinished at the time of his death in 1870.

London looms large throughout Dickens' writing and especially so in novels such as *Bleak House* (1853) and *Our Mutual Friend* (1865), in which the sentiment of Dickens' earlier works gives way to strong social criticism. Dickens' astonishingly broad vision of the city encompassed almost the entire spectrum of London life, effectively defining the city for future generations.

Plot Summary: More than any other of Dickens' gargantuan novels, *Bleak House* resists all attempts at summary. At the heart of this complex web of interwoven stories lies the unresolved lawsuit of Jarndyce and Jarndyce, on whose outcome the family inheritance rests. From this protracted case and the law courts of Chancery Lane where the case is periodically heard, a series of events spirals outward, affecting those myriad characters whose divergent fortunes are, to varying degrees, bound up with the arbitrary and absurd processes of the legal system.

Richard Carstone and Ada Clare are Wards of Court and live with their relative John Jarndyce in the family home of Bleak House. Here they are joined by the novel's heroine and primary narrative voice, the supposed orphan, Esther Summerson. Meanwhile, the aristocratic Lady Dedlock begins the search for her illegitimate child (Esther), a search that leads inexorably to death and disgrace, while elsewhere the mysterious murder of old lawyer Tulkinghorn results in the introduction of Inspector Bucket. Alongside murder and scandal we also witness poverty and degradation in the form of the penniless and illiterate Jo, while love blossoms between Esther and the young Doctor Woodcourt. Needless to say, this love affair does not run smoothly and at one stage Esther is set to marry John Jarndyce before he finally releases her from her engagement. As the novel closes so the lawsuit is finally concluded, only for the inheritance Richard Carstone was expecting to be consumed in legal fees. He dies, but leaves his wife with a son she names Richard. A degree of happiness is finally attained for Esther as she marries Woodcourt, despite having had her beauty marred by the ravages of smallpox.

In-between these episodes are woven numerous other events peopled by a huge cast of minor characters from the comic to the pitiful, and while many of these themes go unresolved and are sometimes inconsistent, Dickens successfully depicts a society that, though appearing outwardly orderly, is in reality chaotic and unpredictable.

Key London Scene: The novel opens with the chapter 'In Chancery' and one of the most evocative descriptions of the city ever penned:

> London. Michaelmas term lately over, and the Lord Chancellor sitting in Lincoln's Inn Hall. Implacable November weather. As much mud in the streets, as if

the waters had but newly retired from the face of the earth, and it would not be wonderful to meet a Megalosaurus, forty feet long or so, waddling like an elephantine lizard up Holborn Hill. Smoke lowering down from chimney-pots, making a soft black drizzle with flakes of soot in it as big as full-grown snowflakes – gone into mourning, one might imagine, for the death of the sun. Dogs, undistinguishable in mire. Horses, scarcely better; splashed to their very blinkers. Foot passengers, jostling one another's umbrellas, in a general infection of ill temper, and losing their foot-hold at street-corners, where tens of thousands of other foot passengers have been slipping and sliding since the day broke (if this day ever broke), adding new deposits to the crust upon crust of mud, sticking at those points tenaciously to the pavement, and accumulating at compound interest.

Evaluation: Bleak House is not an easy book to complete. The plot, as far as there is one, is fragmentary and full of circuitous paths and sudden digressions. In this sense the book itself allegorises both the interminable and unintelligible legal system at its heart, as well as providing a further allegory for the city itself. Such a book is, like the London it mirrors, almost impossible to grasp in its entirety, and while its disjointed and unwieldy form may result from the demands of a serialised publication, it is perfectly suited to its portrayal of the city. This city is organic, but it is an organism that is far from healthy and the recurrent motif of the novel is one of decay and corruption. The body of London is diseased, the smallpox and cholera of the day once again allegorical of wider ills, as the legal and business 'system' actively impoverishes and represses large sections of society. Written at a time when London was an Imperial city that had confidently celebrated its status in the Great Exhibition of 1851, Dickens was able to reveal the human cost of a system that, in elevating a minority to wealth and prestige, condemned the masses to misery and despair.

George Gissing, *New Grub Street* (1891)

Author and Background: Born in Wakefield in 1857, George Gissing was educated at Owens College, Manchester, but was dismissed in 1876 following his theft of money to help the prostitute Nell Harrison, later to become his wife. This unhappy episode was the first of many in a conspicuously miserable life. After serving a month's hard labour, Gissing spent a year in America before returning to pursue a literary career. Years of poverty were to follow along with the death of his wife in 1888, yet despite these setbacks Gissing produced a series of novels, beginning with the publication of *Workers in the Dawn* in 1880. *The Nether World* (1889) attracted some critical attention, but it was with *New Grub Street* (1891) that Gissing's reputation was secured. Further novels include *Born in Exile* (1892), *The Odd Women* (1893), *In the Year of Jubilee* (1894) and *The Crown of Life* (1899). Gissing moved to France in 1899 and died in 1903.

Much of Gissing's work concerns the plight of the urban poor and in his unsentimental depiction of misery and humiliation, *New Grub Street* reads as much as a sociological document as a work of fiction. Heavily influenced by the naturalism of Zola, Gissing's novel captures a cross-section of the literary London of his day and reflects his own position as a struggling writer. Characterised by pessimism and an acute empathy, it was bitterly ironical that Gissing was not to profit from his one acknowledged masterpiece, having sold the copyright for £150. Through his analysis of the divergent forces of the commercial and the creative, Gissing's novel was to be influential on later accounts of literary aspiration in novels such as George Orwell's *Keep the Aspidistra Flying* (1936).

Plot Summary: Gissing's great London novel explores the opposing claims of trade and art in the literary world through the interwoven stories of two quite different couples. Set in the by now familiar, fogbound streets of the late Victorian city, the novel is populated by writers and editors, journalists and agents, caught up in a commercial jungle in which only the successful survive.

Edwin Reardon is a minor novelist with an ambitious wife, Amy. A tortured figure, Edwin's pitiful literary output comes at great cost, both physically and psychologically, and a combination of writer's block and broken health clearly mark him out as a victim of the literary struggle. Jasper Milvain, on the other hand, is a commercially aware journalist who plays the system to his advantage. He is courting Marian Yule, but his emotions are at odds with his plans to marry into money, and so having proposed to Marian on the understanding of an inheritance, he all too quickly retracts this proposal when the money is not forthcoming.

So we witness the divergent fates of these two writers. His work neglected and abandoned by his wife, Reardon's life disintegrates and he soon succumbs to pneumonia. Meanwhile, Jasper rejects Marian in favour of the newly wealthy Amy and in the final irony Jasper publishes a tribute to Reardon's neglected novels.

Alongside these twin narratives is a host of minor characters, from the embittered Alfred Yule, the victim of an unhappy marriage, to Whelpdale the failed novelist cum 'literary adviser' and the miserable figure of Biffen, whose life ends in suicide. All of these figures are made or broken by their literary endeavours in a city blind to their suffering and indifferent to their artistic pretensions.

Key London Scene: As Marian toils away in the reading-room of the British library, she likens her surroundings to a book-lined prison:

The fog grew thicker; she looked up at the windows beneath the dome and saw that they were a dusky yellow. Then her eye discerned an official walking along the upper gallery, and in pursuance of her grotesque humour, her mocking misery, she likened him to a black, lost soul, doomed to wander in an eternity of vain research along endless shelves. Or again, the readers who sat here at these radiating lines of desks, what were they but hapless flies caught in a huge web, its nucleus the great circle of the Catalogue? Darker, darker. From the towering wall of volumes seemed to emanate visible motes, intensifying the obscurity; in a moment the book-lined circumference of the room would be but a featureless prison-limit.

Evaluation: Gissing's work lacks both the humour and the sentiment of Dickens, and while *David Copperfield* describes the struggles of the would-be writer it in no way touches upon the depths of personal disillusionment with which Gissing imbues his tale. This unremitting bleakness can be rather deflating and would appear wilfully morose were it not for the fact that so many of the deprivations recorded here are based upon Gissing's own experiences. *New Grub Street* demonstrates the risks facing the writer choosing to take London as his subject matter. For in recording the emerging figure of the professional writer, Gissing's book is a pioneering account of a time when writers literally starved for their art and in capturing the tortured and sometimes fatal relationship between the writer and the city it has never been surpassed.

Joseph Conrad, *The Secret Agent* (1907)

Author and Background: The facts of Conrad's life are certainly as remarkable as any of his fictional inventions. Born in the Ukraine in 1857 to Polish parents, Jósef Korzeniowski went to sea at the age of 16 and in 1878 joined the English Merchant Marine. Having spent almost 20 years as a sailor, Conrad became a British subject in 1886 and began a career as a full-time writer. Novels such as *Lord Jim* (1900) and *Nostromo* (1904) established his reputation, but critical acclaim was not matched by commercial success and it was not until his later life that Conrad was financially secure. By the time of his death in 1924 Conrad was recognised as a literary giant, his sophisticated tone and complex technique placing him as a bridge between his Victorian forebears and the emergence of literary modernism.

The Secret Agent (1907) is loosely based on a factual event – the explosion that took place in Greenwich Park in 1894, in which the hapless terrorist Martin Bourdin was the only victim. This episode is skilfully woven into a text that explores a city whose darkness reflects the twisted motives of political extremism and whose anonymity provides a home, both then as now, for those unseen figures who move amongst us while plotting our downfall.

Plot Summary: Mr Verloc, his wife Winnie, her elderly mother and idiot brother Stevie run a small shop in Soho selling pornography. Yet behind this squalid exterior Verloc leads something of a double life as an informant and spy moving in a circle of would-be revolutionaries. A fat and lazy man, Verloc's life of espionage takes place mainly through animated conversations with his similarly ineffectual comrades. But having been summoned to a meeting with his controller, the sinister Mr Vladimir, Verloc is persuaded that words must be replaced by action and he is charged with executing a 'bomb outrage' at the Royal Observatory in Greenwich Park.

Soon realising that his circle of misfits is not up to the job, Verloc callously persuades the kind-hearted but simple Stevie to be his accomplice. But his plans go horribly wrong as Stevie fumbles and blows himself up. Hiding the truth from Winnie by claiming that Stevie is visiting relatives in the country, Verloc plans his escape. Soon, however, Chief Inspector Heat is on the case and after discovering a scrap of Stevie's jacket with an address label sewn in, his suspicions fall upon Verloc. Eventually he confronts Verloc with the truth, only for Winnie to overhear his confession. After an attempt to justify his actions, his wife stabs him through the heart. The novel ends with a panic-stricken Winnie turning to Verloc's comrade Ossipon for help, but he betrays her and steals her money; Winnie throws herself overboard while escaping to France on the steamer.

Key London Scene: In Conrad's novel the police are no better than their criminal counterparts, with them all clearly lacking in compassion and understanding. Here, the Assistant Commissioner walks through London's streets revelling in the anonymity they afford:

A pleasurable feeling of independence possessed him when he heard the glass doors swing to behind his back with a sort of imperfect baffled thud. He advanced at once into an immensity of greasy slime and damp plaster interspersed with lamps, and enveloped, oppressed, penetrated, choked, and suffocated by the blackness of a wet London night, which is composed of soot and drops of water.

Brett Street was not very far away. It branched off, narrow, from the side of an open triangular space surrounded by dark and mysterious houses, temples of petty commerce emptied of traders for the night. Only a fruiterer's stall at the corner made a violent blaze of light and colour. Beyond all was black, and the few people passing in that direction vanished at one stride beyond the glowing heaps of oranges and lemons. No footsteps echoed. They would never be heard of again…

Evaluation: In *The Secret Agent*, Conrad demonstrates that *The Heart of Darkness* does not lie in the far reaches of Colonial Africa but closer to home within the streets of Imperial London. Conrad relishes his descriptions of these grotesque characters and his portrayal of the city itself is an equally unattractive portrait of an overcrowded and decaying metropolis. Life in London is characterised by acts of violence and despair and is conducted both cynically and deceitfully with criminal and authority equally culpable. From the familiar squalor of Soho to the opulence of Kensington, London is a site of darkness in which the inequities of Empire are revisited upon the city and in which the savagery that lies beneath the veneer of civilisation is finally revealed.

Virginia Woolf, *Mrs Dalloway* (1925)

Author and Background: Virginia Woolf is the central figure in the intersection between literary modernism and London writing. Born in 1882, a difficult childhood was the prelude to a series of breakdowns and mental ill-health. She married Leonard Woolf in 1912 and together they established the Hogarth Press. Along with figures such as Lytton Strachey, Vanessa Bell and Roger Fry, they formed the literary and artistic circle that came to be known as the Bloomsbury Group. Her first novel, *The Voyage Out*, appeared in 1915 and was followed by an increasingly experimental series of novels that includes *Jacob's Room* (1922), *Orlando* (1928), *The Waves* (1931), *The Years* (1937) and *Between the Acts* (1941). Virginia Woolf committed suicide in 1941.

Much of Woolf's writing was engaged with the city in which she lived, but nowhere is this more apparent than in *Mrs Dalloway* (1925). Using an impressionistic tone to capture the thoughts and sensations of her characters through one summer's day in 1923, Woolf's combination of interior monologue and acute observation vividly realises a single moment in the life of the city while also establishing something of a blueprint for the modernist novel.

Plot Summary: The events recorded in *Mrs Dalloway* take place on a single day – 13 June 1923, and are portrayed principally through the memories and impressions of the novel's heroine, Clarissa Dalloway, the wife of an

MP who is preparing for a dinner party that evening. Elsewhere, Peter Walsh, Clarissa's old lover who has recently returned from India, wanders through the city recalling their relationship and his regret at its ending. Meanwhile, Septimus Smith, a shell-shocked war veteran, is increasingly falling victim to madness as he begins to interpret his surroundings in bizarre and frightening ways. Through the course of this summer's day these lives gradually intersect, and as we learn their thoughts so we see a picture of both their society and the city itself.

As the day passes we are introduced to other characters such as Septimus' wife, Rezia, Clarissa's husband, Richard, and Clarissa's friend, Sally, and through the use of flashbacks we gradually learn their histories and relationships. The novel was originally planned as a series of vignettes and certainly there is little plot as such. But as we follow these characters across the city and alternate between present and past, the comfortable and largely conventional existence of Clarissa Dalloway and her friends is increasingly contrasted with the suffering and delusions of Septimus Smith and his wife, and as the novel ends at Clarissa's dinner party we learn in passing of the suicide of Septimus Smith.

Key London Scene: As we are introduced to Clarissa Dalloway, the sound of Big Ben's chimes reaffirms her love of London:

For having lived in Westminster – how many years now? over twenty, – one feels even in the midst of the traffic, or waking at night, Clarissa was positive, a particular hush, or solemnity; an indescribable pause, a suspense (but that might be her heart, affected, they said, by influenza) before Big Ben strikes. There! Out it boomed. First a warning, musical; then the hour, irrevocable. The leaden circles dissolved in the air. Such fools we are, she thought, crossing Victoria Street. For Heaven only knows why one loves it so, how one sees it so, making it up, building it round one, tumbling it, creating it every moment afresh; but the veriest frumps, the most dejected of miseries sitting on doorsteps (drink their downfall) do the same; can't be dealt with, she felt positive, by Acts of Parliament for that very reason: they love life. In people's eyes, in the swing, tramp, and trudge; in the bellow and the uproar; the carriages, motor cars, omnibuses, vans, sandwich men shuffling and swinging; brass bands; barrel organs; in the triumph and the jingle and the strange high singing of some aeroplane overhead was what she loved; life; London; this moment of June.

Evaluation: Mrs Dalloway can be a difficult book to warm to. It's sophisticated form and acutely rendered observations may demand admiration, but the characters themselves inspire little of the emotional engagement to be found elsewhere in the London Canon. When placed in sequence, *Mrs Dalloway* simply cannot compete with the appalling miseries of some of these earlier novels, and even Septimus Smith's breakdown and suicide are unable to provoke a powerful response.

Perhaps it is the realisation that Woolf's London is rendered here with great depth but little corresponding width that diminishes its appeal. For in its examination of a particularly narrow social class, Clarrisa Dalloway's passionless and conventional existence ultimately seems of surprisingly little consequence.

Evelyn Waugh, *Vile Bodies* (1930)

Author and Background: Evelyn Waugh was born in Hampstead in 1903 into a literary family and was educated at Lancing and Oxford. His first book, a biography of Dante Gabriel Rossetti, was published in 1928. That year also saw the publication of his first novel, *Decline and Fall*, which was followed by *Vile Bodies* (1930), *Black Mischief* (1932), *A Handful of Dust* (1934), *Scoop* (1938) and *Brideshead Revisited* (1945). Waugh travelled widely during these years and also produced a number of travel books. He served in the Army during the war and was to use these experiences as the basis for his *Sword of Honour* trilogy, comprising *Men at Arms* (1952), *Officers and Gentlemen* (1955) and *Unconditional Surrender* (1961). *The Ordeal of Gilbert Pinfold* appeared in 1957. Waugh left London for the West Country where he spent many years with his wife and six children until his death in 1966.

Vile Bodies perfectly captures that short-lived period between the wars when the 'Bright Young Things' of Mayfair lived a hedonistic life of endless partying. Waugh described himself as 'a member rather on the fringe than in the centre', and this distance allowed him to record with a satirical eye an anarchic moment of youthful rebellion.

Plot Summary: Beginning on a turbulent boat crossing to Dover, we are immediately introduced to a bizarre selection of characters, from the Jesuit Father Rothschild and the evangelist Mrs Melrose Ape to Agatha Runcible and Miles Malpractice of the 'Younger Set'. It is to the writer, Adam Fenwick-Symes, however, that much of the novel is devoted and to his inept attempts to raise enough money to secure the hand of his lover, Nina Blount. Once back in England the action moves swiftly to London and to Lottie Crump's hotel in Mayfair, and from here we begin a varied sequence of accidents and embarrassments as the parties move from house to house (memorably including No. 10 Downing St), then from London to the countryside and back. Amidst all this drunken partying the only work that seems to be conducted is that of writing the gossip column for the Daily Excess, a job that is held at one point by most of the characters.

As Adam swings from wealth to poverty chasing a drunken, one-eyed Major who owes him a fortune, so his engagement to Nina remains uncertain and despite his attempts to win over Nina's eccentric father, Colonel Blount, the novel ends with Nina marrying her childhood friend Ginger. Needless to say, none of these events is taken with any seriousness whatsoever and even the novel's conclusion in a gloomy but prescient hint at things to come, as war is declared and

Adam finds himself transported to a desolate battlefield, is handled with customary humour.

Key London Scene: Travelling from bar to bar in search of a party, Mayfair becomes the setting for endless revelry as an unlikely cast of characters try to keep the champagne flowing:

> There were about a dozen people left at the party; that hard kernel of gaiety that never breaks. It was about three o'clock.
>
> "Let's go to Lottie Crump's and have a drink," said Adam. So they all got into two taxicabs and drove across Berkeley Square to Dover Street. But at Shepheard's the night porter said that Mrs Crump had just gone to bed. He thought that Judge Skimp was still up with some friends; would they like to join them? They went up to Judge Skimp's suite, but there had been a disaster there with a chandelier that one of his young ladies had tried to swing on. They were bathing her forehead with champagne; two of them were asleep.
>
> So Adam's party went out again, into the rain.
>
> "Of course, there's always the Ritz," said Archie. "I believe the night porter can usually get one a drink." But he said it in the sort of voice that made all the others say, no, the Ritz was too, too boring at that time of night.
>
> They went to Agatha Runcible's house, which was quite near, but she found that she'd lost her latchkey, so that was no good. Soon some one would say those

fatal words, "Well, I think it's time for me to go to bed. Can I give any one a lift to Knightsbridge?" and the party would be over.

Evaluation: Waugh creates a fantasy London of absurd characters and equally ludicrous events and yet beneath this whimsical surface lies a real time and place, in which Mayfair became a self-contained world. To these extraordinary characters, life is to be lived free from either the traumatic memories of the Great War or anxieties over an uncertain future. For a short-lived period a youthful and privileged few lived purely for the moment and despite Waugh's thankfully outdated prejudices *Vile Bodies* remains a genuinely funny book; indeed, it is something of a welcome relief from the unbroken misery of many London novels.

Occult London

'But the unknown world is, in truth, about us everywhere, everywhere near to our feet; the thinnest veil separates us from it, the door in the wall of the next street communicates with it. There are certain parts of Clapton from which it is possible, on sunny days, to see the pleasant hills of Bleulah, though topographical experts might possibly assure you that it was only Epping Forest. But men of science are always wrong.'

Arthur Machen, *The London Adventure,*
or *The Art of Wandering* (1924)

The Gothic novel has a long tradition within English literary history, from its earliest manifestations in Horace Walpole's *The Castle of Otranto* (1764) and Ann Radcliffe's *The Mysteries of Udolpho* (1794) through to the revival of occult themes in contemporary writers such as Iain Sinclair and Peter Ackroyd.

This tradition intersects with the history of London writing most forcefully during the fin de siècle years of the late nineteenth century when writers such as Robert Louis Stevenson, Oscar Wilde and Arthur Machen immortalised the city as a place of uncanny events and dark secrets. Transposing the Gothic novel to the streets of London, however, required a wholesale reversal in the established norms and techniques of the genre. For while earlier examples invariably lead away from the city towards some isolated and barren location, often in both a distant time and a distant (and usually Catholic) country, the urban Gothic brought these occult events into uncomfortably close proximity to the middle-class respectability of Victorian London, in the process creating an imaginative landscape of labyrinthine streets shrouded in fog that has been the most enduring of all visions of the city.

While Dickens and his popular contemporary GWM Reynolds had themselves produced colourful accounts of life in the 'rookeries' or slums of Victorian London, playing upon the fears of an urban underclass, it was only in the closing years of the century that we witness the more psychological approach of the occult novel, in which the city itself reflects the motives and desires of the characters and itself becomes implicated in these increasingly sensational scenarios. The key motif of these occult fictions is that of the double, leading to both correspondence and conflict at every level of life in the city, from the outward respectability that masks a life of vice and transgression, to a tale of two Londons that sees squalor set against wealth and privilege as the East End becomes an invisible world on the margins of the known city. In this sense, the occult unmasks the hidden city behind the familiar surface and beneath these tales of unnamed vices and bizarre transformations lies an exposure of the dark reality of the lives of many nineteenth-century Londoners.

Yet today London writing has witnessed an occult revival as writers become increasingly preoccupied with the occult themes that characterised the city a century before. In the novels of Iain Sinclair, Peter Ackroyd, Neil Gaiman and numerous others we once again find ourselves within an alternative London, as the familiar streets of the modern-day city become increasingly haunted by the revenants of an earlier age.

Robert Louis Stevenson, *The Strange Case of Dr Jekyll and Mr Hyde* (1886)

Author and Background: Robert Louis Stevenson was born in Edinburgh in 1850 and studied law at Edinburgh University before pursuing a career as a writer. Dogged by illness from an early age, he spent much of his life travelling in search of a climate suitable for his fragile health, eventually settling in Samoa where he died in 1894.

His early novels *Treasure Island* (1883) and *Kidnapped* (1886) established his name as an adventure writer, but it was the publication of *The Strange Case of Dr Jekyll and Mr Hyde* in 1886 that finally gained him critical acclaim. The novel was later dramatised and was playing in Whitechapel at the time of the Ripper murders; withdrawn to avoid giving public offence, it remained forged in the public imagination as a part of the myth of Victorian London alongside the works of Dickens and Conan Doyle.

Originally published as a 'shilling shocker' to catch the Christmas market of 1885, *Jekyll and Hyde* borrows many of the conventions of the detective novel. In trawling through the often insalubrious streets of the city it portrays a London at odds with the respectable middle-class conventions of the day, offering the reader an uncomfortably close look at the darker side of the individual, society and the city itself.

Plot Summary: Mr Utterson, Dr Jekyll's lawyer and friend, is told the story of how a man called Hyde is witnessed knocking down and trampling a small child. On being approached, Hyde is forced to offer reparation to the child's family and is seen entering Dr Jekyll's house by a disused rear entrance before returning with a cheque bearing Jekyll's name. Utterson, troubled by Dr Jekyll's new will, which leaves his entire estate to Hyde, becomes intrigued and, suspecting blackmail, decides to investigate the matter further.

Watching the rear door of Jekyll's house, Utterson eventually meets Hyde and obtains his address in Soho, and a fortnight later, following the brutal murder of Sir Danvers Carew, he leads the police to Soho and Hyde's disreputable life is exposed. Hyde disappears, however, and his trail soon goes cold.

Some time later, Dr Lanyon, a friend of Jekyll's, calls upon Utterson and passes him a letter to be opened only in the event of Jekyll's death. Lanyon himself dies shortly after and soon Jekyll himself is taken ill and is seemingly confined to his rooms. Utterson becomes suspicious and having been visited by Jekyll's servant Poole, they both return to Jekyll's house, where on breaking into his rooms they are confronted by the body of Hyde. Jekyll is missing and presuming him murdered by Hyde, Utterson opens Dr Lanyon's letter and the whole mystery is unravelled.

Lanyon reveals how on visiting Hyde with a strange drug he requested him to bring, he witnesses Hyde's terrible transformation back into Henry Jekyll. Jekyll and Hyde are the same man and the novel closes with Jekyll's written account of the experiments that first released the evil embodied by Hyde and how subsequently he begins to dominate his own personality. In the ensuing struggle to rid himself of Hyde, Jekyll is forced to commit suicide.

Key London Scene: Following the murder of Sir Danvers Carew, Utterson leads the police to Soho in search of the home of Edward Hyde:

It was by this time about nine in the morning, and the first fog of the season. A great chocolate-coloured pall lowered over heaven, but the wind was continually charging and routing these embattled vapours; so that as the cab crawled from street to street, Mr Utterson beheld a marvellous number of degrees and hues of twilight; for here it would be dark like the back-end of evening; and there would be a glow of a rich, lurid brown, like the blight of some strange conflagration; and here, for a moment, the fog would be quite broken up, and a haggard shaft of daylight would glance in between the swirling wreaths. The dismal quarter of Soho seen under these changing glimpses, with its muddy ways, and slatternly passengers, and its lamps which had never been extinguished or had been kindled afresh to combat this mournful reinvasion of darkness, seemed, in the lawyer's eyes, like a district of some city in a nightmare...

As the cab drew up before the address indicated, the fog lifted a little and showed him a dingy street, a gin palace, a low French eating house, a shop for the retail of penny numbers and twopenny salads, many ragged children huddled in the doorways, and many women of many different nationalities passing out, key in hand, to have a morning glass; and the next moment the fog settled down again upon that part, as brown as umber, and cut him off from his blackguardly surroundings. This was the home of Henry Jekyll's favourite; of a man who was heir to a quarter of a million sterling.

Evaluation: The London portrayed here is a largely allegorical one without the specificities of actual London settings, and just as Hyde is the disreputable element masked by Jekyll's respectable exterior, so too does Hyde's home in Soho itself become the hidden site of squalid degeneracy amidst the wealth and privilege of London's West End. For with its grand façade disguising the rather squalid rear entrance, Jekyll's house mirrors the layout of the city in which poverty existed in tandem with wealth but remained carefully concealed from view.

The city of Jekyll and Hyde is not simply the setting for occult practices, but like so many of the novels of the London occult, is itself bound up with the actions to which it plays host. For the swirling fog seems to resist the investigations of the police, helping to obscure Hyde and his crimes and shrouding those parts of Victorian London that many of its inhabitants preferred not to acknowledge. In this sense, the novel provides a template for later investigations of the city, creating a mythical image so powerful that it foreshadows many of the novels that were to follow.

Arthur Machen, *The Great God Pan* (1894)

Author and Background: Written just eight years after *Jekyll and Hyde*, Arthur Machen's first novel explores many of the same themes without achieving anything like the lasting influence of Stevenson's work. Born in 1863 at Caerleon, Arthur Machen spent his childhood deep within the Welsh countryside and, despite moving to London, where he remained for most of his life, much of his writing is pervaded by the mystical land-scapes of his youth. Commissioned to compile a defin-itive catalogue of occult literature, Machen's lasting interest in occult matters colours almost all his work, inspiring a stream of novels, treatises and biographical works. The first, and best known of these, is his novel *The Great God Pan*, which was published to generally hostile reviews in 1894. Today its decadent themes may appear laughably tame, but at the time they roused one critic to describe the novel as 'an incoherent nightmare of sex'. Machen remains very much on the margins of literary history, but he holds a more substantial position within the history of London writing, where, alongside *The Great God Pan*, later novels such as *The Three Impostors* (1895) and his autobiographical tale of London walking, *The London Adventure,* or *The Art of Wandering* (1924), have maintained a lasting influence.

Machen continued to write until his death in 1947, at the age of 84. Having outlived the Gothic flowering of his youth, he provides an important link with later occultists such as his fellow members of the Golden Dawn, WB Yeats and Aleister Crowley. It is as a London writer, however, that he is primarily remembered and for his depiction of the 'Ars Magna of London' – that enchanted city which he saw as a self-contained universe of unceasing wonder and delight.

Plot Summary: In the country home of Dr Raymond, an operation is performed which attempts to remove the veil between the worlds of reality and dream. The experiment fails and the girl Mary, Raymond's adopted daughter, is left a hopeless idiot.

Many years later Clarke, present at these events and now returned to London, is writing his memoirs and recounting details of a Helen V., who is seen playing with a 'strange naked man' in the Welsh countryside and who inspires such terror in a small boy that he is rendered insensible. It soon becomes apparent that this lady is the daughter of the girl Mary, spawned nine months after the failed experiment and now it would seem possessed by some diabolical power.

The narrative switches to the streets of Soho where a friend of Clarke's, named Villiers, stumbles across an old acquaintance now reduced to begging on the street. As it turns out, this friend Herbert was married to Helen, who, having 'corrupted his soul', left him broken and destitute. Herbert is found dead some weeks later apparently from starvation and soon the tale of Helen Vaughan comes out and with it a trail of broken and traumatised men who die in mysterious circumstances. Villiers is urged by Clarke to forget about Helen, as he suspects the monstrous truth of her real identity, but, undeterred, Villiers determines to find her. About this time a series of suicides begins amongst well-to-do gentlemen and Villiers soon discovers that Helen has returned to London. Under the alias of Mrs Beaumont, she is luring these men to their deaths through an unspecified mixture of frenzied lust and horror that results in their inevitable suicide. Now living in Piccadilly, the novel closes with Villiers and Clarke setting out to her home armed with a noose that they intend to offer her as an alternative to arrest. The full horror of this final episode is narrated by the doctor who witnesses the scene, as Helen, on the point of death, is horribly transformed into a blackened jelly before finally expiring.

Key London Scene: Walking through Soho one evening, Villiers comes across his old friend Herbert, now a destitute beggar. Taking his arm, they set off together through the streets:

The ill-assorted pair moved slowly up Rupert Street; the one in dirty, evil-looking rags, the other attired in the regulation uniform of a man about town, trim, glossy, and eminently well-to-do. Villiers had emerged from his restaurant after an excellent dinner of many courses, assisted by an ingratiating little flask of Chianti, and, in that frame of mind which was with him almost chronic, had delayed a moment by the door, peering round in the dimly lighted street in search of those mysterious incidents and persons with which the streets of London teem in every quarter and at every hour. Villiers prided himself as a practised explorer of such obscure mazes and byways of London life, and in this unprofitable pursuit he displayed an assiduity which was worthy of more serious employment. Thus he stood beside the lamp-post surveying the passers-by with undisguised curiosity, and with that gravity only known to the systematic diner, had just enunciated in his mind the formula: 'London has been called the city of encounters; it is more than that, it is the city of resurrections.'

Evaluation: Machen's novel lacks the coherence and inventiveness of *Dr Jekyll and Mr Hyde* and while the two novels employ similar themes – the experiment gone wrong, the hints of sexual and moral depravity and the use of letters to reveal key elements of the plot – their treatment of London is quite different. For while Stevenson paints an allegorical image of the city obscured by fog, Machen's London is given clear coordinates and specific locations and one can recognise the voice of Machen himself in those instances when the characters philosophise upon the nature of the city as they walk. Soho once again becomes the site of depravity and mystery, but for Machen the city is open to whoever wishes to explore its streets.

Peter Ackroyd, *Hawksmoor* (1985)

Author and Background: Born in 1949, Peter Ackroyd was brought up in London before attending Cambridge and Yale. He returned to London to pursue a career as a journalist and having published several collections of poetry and criticism, he turned to fiction with *The Great Fire of London* (1982). He has since produced a series of London novels including *The Last Testament of Oscar Wilde* (1983), *The House of Doctor Dee* (1993), *Dan Leno and the Limehouse Golem* (1994) and most recently *The Lambs of London* (2004). These novels often combine historical re-enactment with an exploration of the occult, and offer a twofold perspective of the city through the conflict between rational and irrational forces. Elsewhere, Ackroyd has written of two opposing strands within English cultural tradition, in which the rational forces of the Enlightenment have come to suppress the more mystical or visionary elements of Catholic culture represented by 'Cockney Visionaries' such as Blake and Dickens, who were able to perceive the eternal and unchanging fabric of the city behind the superficial flux of everyday life.

It is this conflict that forms the ideological backdrop to *Hawksmoor* and in this novel Ackroyd dramatises the struggle between the occult tradition and the New Science of eighteenth-century thought through the depiction of a series of murders that are linked with the occult significance of Hawksmoor's London churches. Yet Ackroyd's descriptions of occult practices must be read alongside his portrayal of London in the 1980s – a drab and anonymous setting of poverty and violence that inevitably introduces a political dimension to the novel and questions the role of Thatcherism in refashioning the city.

Plot Summary: The novel is structured by alternating chapters as the narrative switches from the London of Queen Anne to the present day. We begin in 1711, when, following a commission to build a series of churches across the city, Nicholas Dyer (taking on Hawksmoor's historical role) begins work as an assistant to Sir Christopher Wren. It soon becomes clear that Dyer follows an occult philosophy opposed to the scientific approach of Wren and both the design and sites of his churches are charged with an occult meaning concealed from his master. As the novel progresses, this occult agenda leads to several murders as a series of victims are offered up as sacrifices to Dyer's dark designs. These murders and almost every event in the narrative are echoed in the modern day London of 1985. Here, too, children and vagrants fall victim to a killer whose murders follow the locations of Hawksmoor's churches.

The second part of the novel introduces us to Detective Chief Superintendent Hawksmoor, whose job it is to apprehend the killer and whose own increasingly bizarre behaviour distances him from his more conventional colleagues. Soon Hawksmoor begins to comprehend the significance of the occult settings and begins to search for a vagrant known as the Architect, who appears to be responsible for the killings. As the novel progresses the identities of Dyer and Hawksmoor begin to merge as the time and space that separates them begins to collapse. In the novel's rather incoherent conclusion the inevitable meeting of Hawksmoor and Dyer becomes a spiritual union as these characters become one. With the circle complete we are returned to the beginning as the cycle of murderer and victim begins once again.

Key London Setting: Walking through a bleak and blackened landscape of deserted buildings peopled by vagrants, Hawksmoor approaches Wapping and muses upon the tendency of murderers and their victims to return repeatedly to the same areas of the city:

Hawksmoor could have produced a survey of the area between the two churches of Wapping and Limehouse, and given at the same time a precise account of the crimes each quarter harboured... He grew to understand that most criminals tend to remain in the same districts, continuing with their activities until they were arrested, and he sometimes speculated that these same areas had been used with similar intent for centuries past: even murderers, who rapidly became Hawksmoor's speciality, rarely moved from the same spot but killed again and again until they were discovered. And sometimes he speculated, also, that they were drawn to those places where murders had occurred before… And it did not take any knowledge of the even more celebrated Whitechapel murders, all of them conducted around Christ Church, Spitalfields, to understand, as Hawksmoor did, that certain streets or patches of ground provoked a malevolence which generally seemed to be quite without motive. And he knew, also, how many murders go undetected and how many murderers remain unknown.

Evaluation: In his *London: The Biography* (2000), Ackroyd examines the idea that there are areas within London that are subject to peculiar temporal and spatial conditions, arguing that these places remain throughout the centuries sites of similar activities and events as history is continuously replayed. This occult theory forms the basis to *Hawksmoor*, in which parallel historical narratives unfold in tandem to emphasise the way in which London's inhabitants, be they vagrants or murderers, often return to reoccupy earlier sites and to repeat earlier events. These historical synchronicities are apparent everywhere to Ackroyd, and reveal a city of unbroken continuity underlying the superficial perception of a city in constant flux. Yet in his depiction of the city in 1985 Ackroyd's London seems to have lost all the vitality and mystery with which he recreates the past. *Hawksmoor* seems to contrast the city of the eighteenth century with its modern day counterpart, describing the latter, in varying shades of grey, as a windswept city of poverty and detritus, populated by an ever-growing underclass subject to violence and despair. It is difficult to dismiss these changes as merely cosmetic and despite Ackroyd's insistence that the present is merely the past revisited, there is little evidence here of an eternal city beneath the concrete. Instead the novel appears to reveal London at a point in its history where it is attempting to sever all links with its past, in the process abandoning those people who are unable or unwilling to participate in the new city that is to replace it.

Iain Sinclair, *White Chappell Scarlet Tracings* (1987)

Author and Background: Born in Wales, and educated at Trinity College, Dublin, Iain Sinclair has lived in London for more than 30 years. In the 1970s he began to produce a series of poems and documentary works taking London as his subject and which were often published by his own Albion Village Press. *Lud Heat* (1975) first proposed the occult alignment of Hawksmoor's churches that was later to be developed by Ackroyd. His first novel, *White Chappell Scarlet Tracings*, was published in 1987. Later novels such as *Downriver* (1991) brought him further acclaim and today he is most widely known for his accounts of a series of walks conducted in and around the city in *Lights Out for the Territory* (1997) and *London Orbital* (2001). Sinclair's work is almost impossible to classify, interweaving poetry with prose, fiction with biography. Alongside Peter Ackroyd, he forms the axis upon which much London writing currently revolves. Collaborations with writers and filmmakers such as JG Ballard and Stewart Home, Chris Petit and Patrick Keiller place him at the centre of a 'London Project', which is often retrospective in scope, rediscovering writers and texts from earlier London traditions. *White Chappell Scarlet Tracings* returns to the myths and imagery of the late Victorian city. The uncanny juxtapositions and occult connections that this creates, blending history and fiction with autobiographical scenes from Sinclair's own life, can make Sinclair's texts impenetrably allusive, with the result that the act of reading becomes a case of deciphering the meaning hidden beneath this obscure surface. In this respect, Sinclair's work ultimately comes to resemble the city it is describing – an accumulation of myths and memories, digressive, chaotic, incoherent but always stimulating.

Plot Summary: The plot of Sinclair's novel completely eludes summary and may best be described in terms of a number of threads that predominate within it. The first of these concerns a renegade band of book dealers who criss-cross the city and the country in pursuit of a hitherto unknown first printing of Conan Doyle's *A Study in Scarlet*. This world is a reworking of Sinclair's own experiences as a book dealer and provides access to a myriad selection of obscure texts that develop an extra-literary existence on the margins of this novel. Elsewhere scenes from Sinclair's experiences as a labourer in the East End come to the fore, but these autobiographical strands repeatedly give way to a meditation upon the Ripper murders through a fictional account of Victorian surgeon and Ripper suspect, William Gull. In these episodes the streets of the Dickensian East End are superimposed upon their contemporary counterparts to create a series of narrative intersections between Gull, Holmes, Sinclair himself and the world of books in which they all meet. The result is a series of distorted images in which the past is viewed through the prism of the present, and in which individual lives become inseparable from the city and its accumulated history.

Key London Setting: As Sinclair's text unfolds we are gradually given the precise coordinates of the world he is exploring, as those streets haunted by the Ripper are conjoined with Sinclair's own experiences of the modern city:

> The zone was gradually defined, the labyrinth penetrated. It was given limits by the victims of the Ripper: the Roebuck and Brady Street in the East, Mitre Square to the West, the Minories to the South, the North largely unvisited. Circling and doubling back, seeing the same sites from different angles, ferns breaking the stones, horses tethered on waste lots, convolvulus swallowing the walls, shadowed by tall tenements, chickens' feet in damp cardboard boxes, entrails of radio sets, slogans on the railway bridge, decayed synagogues, the flash and flutter, cardamom

seeding, of the coming bazaar culture, the first whispers of a new Messiah.

Evaluation: 'We are retrospective,' claims Sinclair, 'Even the walls are soaked with earlier texts, aborted histories.' And the novel supports this claim through its recognition of the fact that all writing is ultimately rewriting. Through this process Sinclair unearths and revives an entire tradition of London writing and takes his place within it.

This sense of the ways in which urban space resonates with the histories of earlier inhabitants and events has been labelled psychogeography and has its roots in the theories of the Situationist movement of the 1950s. It has been defined as 'the study of the specific effects of the geographical environment, conspicuously organised or not, on the emotions and behaviour of individuals'. While it no longer expresses the political radicalism of its origins, psychogeography retains widespread currency amongst contemporary London writers, from Sinclair and Ackroyd to Stewart Home, Christopher Petit and Nicholas Royle.

Sinclair's fiction is far less accessible than his documentary writing because it is a hybrid form in which nothing appears to be discarded. Sinclair's own experiences of the city, his experiences of other fictional accounts of the city, his own fictional and poetic preoccupations, as well as his awareness of the historical, cultural and political background, are all thrown in, often in a seemingly haphazard way, and then presented in a self-consciously poetic form. This results in a text that can present the reader with serious difficulties, but also one that offers the gratifying sense of having consumed an entire library. For each Sinclair book seems to contain within it the entire tradition that preceded it, encapsulating in its many layers a vertical descent through London's literary past.

Neil Gaiman, *Neverwhere* (1996)

Author and Background: Neil Gaiman was born and raised in the UK and has been writing for more than 20 years. His graphic novel sequence, *The Sandman*, was hugely successful, as was his novel *Neverwhere*, which was broadcast as a TV series by the BBC before being released as a novel in 1996. Other books include *American Gods* (2001) and the children's novel *Coraline* (2002). Gaiman now lives in Minneapolis in the USA.

Neverwhere, like many fables of an alternative reality, uses the existence of this other world to highlight the failings of our own, and as in other occult novels such as *Hawksmoor* it is the figure of the vagrant whose invisible existence allows him to act as the gatekeeper to this hidden city. In fact, with their unseen lives in the midst of our own and their use of obscure rituals and locations, it is the London underclass that may be the most natural representatives of a secret city, a city whose secrets may be all too easily revealed to those unfortunate enough to slip through the cracks linking their world with our own.

Plot Summary: Richard Mayhew is walking through

London one evening when he finds a young girl lying injured on the pavement. At her request he takes her to his home and his life is transformed forever. The girl's name is Door and she comes from the Underside, a parallel London beneath the city, and she brings in her wake Mr Croup and Mr Vandermar, two Gothically attired assassins hired to kill her. Having unwittingly entered her world, Richard soon finds himself invisible and isolated within his own as his stable life of girl-friend, job and flat evaporates around him. Determined to regain his old existence, he hunts out Door and through a meeting with a vagrant finds himself in the Underside, a bizarre combination of medieval, Gothic and modern London populated by a cast of grotesque and bizarre characters from talking rats to a dandified aristocrat named the Marquis De Carabas. Soon Richard is reunited with Door and, accompanied by Carabas and a knife-wielding killer called Hunter, they set out to discover who has ordered their murder. What follows is a series of fantastic adventures as they travel between London above and below, facing a number of challenges and meeting a series of characters corre-sponding to famous London locations such as the Angel Islington, Lady Serpentine and Old Bailey. Eventually it becomes clear that there is an ancient evil beneath the city, which, having been incarcerated for centuries, is now planning to escape and take control of the city. To prevent his victory Richard and Door travel deep underground, where, after a final battle, the Angel Islington and his evil henchmen Croup and Vandemar are defeated and Richard is allowed to return to his former life. Yet having resumed his previous existence Richard finds it empty and meaningless and is finally allowed to return to the Underside.

Key London Scene: Having moved to London from Scotland three years before, Richard gradually comes to comprehend the city and to recognise its contradictory nature:

Three years in London had not changed Richard, although it had changed the way he perceived the city. Richard had originally imagined London as a grey city, even a black city, from pictures he had seen, and he was surprised to find it full of colour. It was a city of red brick and white stone, red buses and large black taxis (which were often, to Richard's initial puzzlement, gold, or green, or maroon), bright red post-boxes, and green grassy parks and cemeteries.

It was a city in which the very old and the awkwardly new jostled each other, not uncomfortably, but without respect; a city of shops and offices and restaurants and homes, of parks and churches, of ignored monuments and remarkably unpalatial palaces; a city of hundreds of districts with strange names – Crouch End, Chalk Farm, Earl's Court, Marble Arch – and oddly distinct identities; a noisy, dirty, cheerful, troubled city, which fed on tourists, needed them as it despised them, in which the average speed of transportation through the city had not increased in three hundred years, following five hundred years of fitful road-widening and unskilful compromises between the needs of the traffic, whether horse-drawn, or, more recently, motorised, and the needs of pedestrians; a city inhabited by and teeming with people of every colour and manner and kind.

Evaluation: Gaiman's novel is ceaselessly inventive and paints a beguiling picture of a London much more exciting and alive than our own. Like *Hawksmoor* before it, however, *Neverwhere* feels more at home within the London of the author's imagination than it does in its portrayal of the real city, which merely becomes a rather drab and predictable backdrop. In this sense, these two novels are at odds with the fictions of Machen and Sinclair, both of which identify occult significance within the seemingly mundane surfaces of their own surroundings. Gaiman's fable invests so heavily in its portrayal of the Underside, that the London above the surface is drained of colour and for this reason the distance between these two Londons finally appears too great for Gaiman's world to intrude sufficiently and convincingly upon our own.

London in Ruins

'Hell is a city much like London – A populous and smoky city.'
Percy Bysshe Shelley,
'Peter Bell the Third' (1839)

Writing on the subject of ruined London, the critic Patrick Parrinder recalls Edmund Spenser's *The Ruines of Time* (1590) in which a woman wails on the banks of the Thames as she mourns the destruction of the Roman city of Verulamium, now St Albans, and relocated through poetic licence from Hertfordshire to the Thames Valley.

Today it seems unlikely that the destruction of St Albans would generate such emotion, and yet Spenser's poem is symbolic of an English tradition that finds a home amidst the ruins of abandoned cities. Such images of past splendour now reduced to rubble are perhaps most closely associated with the Romantic depiction of Ancient Rome and Greece, but London itself has its own tradition of those who have visualised its premature demise. Yet the novels that I shall be examining here contain much more than simply an orgy of destructive pleasure, revealing as they do both the prevailing anxieties of their times, as well as visions of a better, or perhaps less favourable, future. Nor are the consequences of London's apocalyptic end necessarily unpleasant, at least in the short term, as the protagonists often find themselves in the enviable position of having the city almost to themselves. In such situations, these characters, believing themselves to be the last men (these figures are almost invariably men) alive tend to respond to this undiluted freedom in an entirely predictable fashion – a looting spree for luxury goods and vintage wines followed by a retreat to a five-star hotel.

In its Victorian form, however, it was exactly this notion of unfettered consumerism, coupled with fears of degenerate vice, an exploding population and the filth and squalor of an urban underclass that made the city ripe for a dramatic makeover, and in most instances this involved a return to a pre-industrial past. The arrival of science fiction simply provided the tools to do a more thorough job of dismantling the city and allowed novelists to describe the process of destruction in a way that earlier fictions tended to side-step through the hazy intervention of a dream. In addition, technological advance allowed the city to be instantly rebuilt and in a more orderly and futuristic manner. For London's essentially medieval layout of labyrinthine streets has long been the target of those dreaming of a more classically proportioned city of cleanly mathematical dimensions.

All the novels featured in this chapter engage in a speculative account of some future calamity, with one exception – less than fifty years after HG Wells' Martians were transforming the city into a smoking ruin, the Luftwaffe was to make this nightmare a reality and so I have included Henry Green's *Caught* (1943) as an example of apocalyptic scenes of destruction based upon fact rather than fiction.

The arrival of the nuclear age and the Cold War produced a new generation of imaginative disasters for the city, but now of course such disasters were only too real in the minds of many and the Disaster Novel formed a sub-genre that played specifically on these fears. Writers such as John Wyndham, most famously in *The Day of the Triffids* (1951), which itself contains images of an abandoned London, and JG Ballard devised ever more ingenious scenarios for the collapse of the human race. As current fears of climate change and global warming emerge, we have gone full circle and have, like the Victorians before us, placed our hopes in a greener future. For in the end, as the following novels demonstrate, our hopes and fears for the city tend to be repeated from one generation to the next, united largely by the belief that barring unforeseen disaster the city will survive and may perhaps even improve.

Richard Jefferies, *After London*, or *Wild England* (1885)

Author and Background: Richard Jefferies (1848–87) was born in Wiltshire and grew up in the countryside, the son of a dairy farmer. Having begun work upon a provincial newspaper he soon moved to London to take up a literary career, initially making his mark with autobiographical accounts of his rural childhood.

After London was first published in 1885, shortly before Jefferies' death from tuberculosis, and has little in common with other futuristic visions of the late Victorian era, such as Samuel Butler's *Erewhon* (1872) and Bulwer-Lytton's *The Coming Race* (1883). For *After London* resists the optimistic faith in human progress that these books present, instead offering a pessimistic outline of the industrial failings of the present alongside an equally demoralising account of the rural alternatives, and it is perhaps for this reason that Jefferies' novel has remained in a state of literary neglect.

In its depiction of the catastrophic demise of the city followed by gradual regression to a rural existence and the inevitable return to survey London in ruins, Jefferies establishes many of the now familiar patterns of the disaster novel. Yet this pioneering example remains perhaps the most virulently anti-urban of all subsequent novels in this tradition, forsaking those romantic images of overgrown buildings for a blackened swamp of noxious fumes, a London that literally drowns under the weight of generations of accumulated waste.

Plot Summary: The novel is divided into two parts, the first of which offers an account of the 'relapse into Barbarism' that follows London's demise. The cause of this catastrophe is unclear – an 'unknown orb' somehow disrupts Earth's magnetic currents – but its effects are meticulously detailed as society collapses and regresses to small rural communities, leaving the cities to disintegrate as mankind gradually discards the learning of previous generations. In this new Dark Age, Southern England is largely under water, leaving the polluted remnants of London cut off from its neighbours and festering under a cloud of poisonous gas.

The second part of the novel is a more straightforward narrative employing all the devices of a courtly romance, albeit one that lacks the correspondingly chivalrous notions of human nature. Felix Aquila is a nobleman living in a small community that has much in common with medieval feudalism, relying largely upon hunting and warfare. Yet Felix is a sensitive and disgruntled youth who aspires to escape the limitations of his society and to marry Aurora, the girl he loves. To do this he needs to impress her family and so he decides to build a canoe, sail across the lake and make his fortune. Having set off, he has a number of experiences and adventures, almost all of which are unpleasant and unrewarding until eventually he finds himself entering the polluted cloud of old London. Here, he is almost overcome by the fatal gases. However, he manages to escape this blackened hell to eventually arrive at a community of shepherds, where, through his masterful use of the bow and arrow, he becomes their leader. But he soon tires of his new companions and the novel ends as he embarks on the long journey home.

Key London Scene: Finding himself drifting through blackened waters, Felix eventually reaches land. Discovering the decaying remnants of earlier inhabitants, he realises that he has found the polluted remains of London:

These skeletons were the miserable relics of men who had ventured, in search of ancient treasures, into the deadly marshes over the site of the mightiest city of former days. The deserted and utterly extinct city of London was under his feet.

He had penetrated into the midst of that dreadful place, of which he had heard many a tradition: how the earth was poison, the water poison, the air poison, the very light of heaven, falling through such an atmosphere, poison. There were said to be places where the earth was on fire and belched forth sulphurous fumes, supposed to be from the combustion of the enormous stores of strange and unknown chemicals collected by the wonderful people of these times. Upon the surface of the water there was a greenish-yellow oil, to touch which was death to any creature; it was the very essence of corruption.

Evaluation: Jefferies' novel is by no means as accomplished as those of many of his contemporaries, and yet what he lacks in literary style he makes up for with the peculiarity of his vision. The plot of *After London* is conventional to the point of being mundane and none of the characters is particularly inspired – he is much more successful in rendering a truly bleak and disturbing picture of the city as it dissolves into a polluted soup, and in resisting the fashions of his day that suggested an onward but inevitably upward struggle for mankind. In this capacity Jefferies was truly ahead of his time in grasping the true implications of Darwinism that man and the civilisation he has built are only temporary and progress is no more assured than regression.

William Morris, *News From Nowhere* (1890)

Author and Background: William Morris (1834–96) was born into wealth and privilege and like many of such background soon developed a taste for radical Socialism. Educated at Marlborough and Oxford, Morris was something of a Renaissance Man, who not only published poetry and translations from Icelandic literature, but was also a leading light in the Arts and Crafts movement and is best remembered today for his commercial designs. Having helped to form the Socialist League in 1884, Morris' belief in equality was combined with a reaction against his perception of the ugliness of the modern world, and it is these twin motifs that inform his utopian fantasy, *News From Nowhere* (1890).

Morris completely dispensed with any economic world view in favour of a highly personal aesthetic and artistic philosophy, which regarded industry with some distaste in preference for a rustic vision of handicrafts and haymaking that owes much to his idiosyncratic view of the Middle Ages. Morris was brought up, in some grandeur, in Walthamstow (then a village in rural Essex) and repeatedly railed against the growth of 'cockneyfied' suburbia that threatened and was soon to overrun London's eastern borders. Toward the end of his life he lived in Hammersmith, a location that features in *News From Nowhere* and in many respects encapsulates everything he disliked about urban life. For ultimately Morris saw the Victorian city as something of an aberration, a historical mistake which, if only corrected, could return us to the rural simplicity of an earlier age. In this belief in a future that is a return to a golden past, Morris is a direct descendant of William Blake, who also saw the need first to destroy London if it were to be rebuilt as a Jerusalem in England's green and pleasant land.

Plot Summary: Returning from a discussion about the revolutionary future to the 'shabby London suburb' of Hammersmith, the narrator falls asleep only to awake more than 200 years later. Winter has given way to glorious sunshine and London has been transformed into what appears to be a recreation of the fourteenth century, populated by friendly and attractive locals dressed in embroidered cloth. The pollution that he remembers has been replaced by cleanliness and the Thames is now clear and well-stocked with salmon. The narrator is greeted by this new race of Londoners and taken on a guided tour of the city, where he soon discovers that the age of industrial development has been reversed. Houses have been cleared and replaced by woodland, the remaining buildings conforming to simple medieval designs and a new life of creative leisure based upon arts and crafts and healthy outdoor pursuits has been established. Alongside this recreation of the built environment, society itself has been equally transformed, with the government of the late nineteenth century giving way to an anarchic freedom regulated by communal halls or 'motes' dispensing a homespun philosophy of equality and self-improvement.

During his brief two-day stay, the narrator is taken around the old West End from Bloomsbury to Westminster, where he witnesses the changes that have been wrought upon the city. Though the narrator constantly questions what he sees, he is unable to establish the existence of any flaws in these new arrangements and his confident nineteenth-century outlook is repeatedly shown to be childishly misguided. His journey is extended to include a boat trip along the Thames and here he learns that the 'cockney villas' that Morris so despised have been swept away and replaced with rolling meadows. After witnessing a final burst of haymaking, his dream comes to an end and he finds himself back in Hammersmith. He is understandably depressed at first, but as the book ends this gives way to an optimistic pledge to work to make his dream a reality.

Key London Scene: As the narrator is taken on a tour of the city he travels through Westminster and on passing the Houses of Parliament he enquires as to their current usage. He receives the following answer:

I take you, neighbour; you may well wonder at our keeping them standing, and I know something about that, and my old kinsman has given me books to read about the strange game that they played there. Use them! Well, yes, they are used for a sort of subsidiary market, and a storage place for manure, and they are handy for that, being on the water-side. I believe it was intended to pull them down quite at the beginning of our days; but there was, I am told, a queer antiquarian society, which had done some service in past times, and which straightway set up its pipe against their destruction, as it has done with many other buildings, which most people looked upon as worthless, and public nuisances; and it was so energetic, and had such good reasons to give, that it generally gained its point; and I must say that when all is said I am glad of it: because you know at the worst these silly old buildings serve as a foil to the beautiful ones which we build now. You will see several others in these parts; the place my great-grandfather lives in, for instance, and a big building called St Paul's.

Evaluation: It is easy to point out the impracticalities of Morris' vision and as a dream of Socialism it is certainly not one that Marx would recognise. Indeed, Engels described Morris as a 'sentimental Socialist', and it is this sentiment and its rather cloying expression that can make *News From Nowhere* slightly irritating. One suspects that an inhabitant of industrialised London could only take so much of the simple wisdom dispensed by these constantly blushing and unfailingly good-humoured farmhands before responding violently against their carefully thatched and attractively decorated environment. At one point, upon hearing that the entire world has embraced this new creed, the narrator questions whether such a lack of variety isn't rather dull and after two days in Morris' paradise one feels that we have already exhausted all the possibilities this new society has to offer.

HG Wells, *The War of the Worlds* (1898)

Author and Background: HG Wells (1866–1946) was brought up in Bromley, Kent, and escaped a life of drudgery through a scholarship to the Normal School of Science in Kensington where he studied under TH Huxley. After stints as a teacher, Wells began to produce the 'scientific romances' for which he is now famous, including *The Time Machine* (1895), *The Island of Dr Moreau* (1896) and *The Invisible Man* (1897). He also wrote a number of largely autobiographical novels such as *Love and Mr Lewisham* (1900) and *Kipps* (1905), which espoused many of his controversial views upon political and sexual liberation. Like Morris before him, Wells was politically active and an early member of the Fabian Society, but while Morris espoused a utopian optimism, Wells offered a more ambiguous vision of the future, his cautionary tales displaying both a belief in technological progress and an awareness of its inherent dangers. While many of his novels have London settings, it is *The War of the Worlds* that offers the most vivid images of apocalyptic London and it is this novel, with its descriptions of a ruthless colonising force subduing a helpless population, that continues to have the greatest relevance today.

Plot Summary: Unknowingly monitored by an alien intelligence, Earth continues happily unaware of the mounting threat from its distant neighbour, Mars. Soon, however, a strange cylinder arrives, landing rather incongruously on Horsell Common near Woking. Following the emergence of its alien passenger, the first curious bystanders are dispatched with its deadly heat ray. The narrator escapes the massacre, but gradually Surrey is gripped by panic and after a series of inadequate attempts to destroy the creature it becomes clear that Earth is under attack.

As the Martians increase in numbers and begin to roam the countryside on huge tripods, the population flees northward towards London. But the Martians' inexorable advance is barely checked by the military and soon Woking, Weybridge and Shepperton have all been reduced to cinders and London itself is threatened.

Meanwhile, our narrator has escaped the destruction and is vainly attempting to reach Leatherhead to find his wife, but has become saddled with a hapless curate whose Christian interpretation of the coming apocalypse is mercilessly ridiculed.

As London is invaded the narrative switches to the narrator's brother, who witnesses the growing panic and mass exodus as six million Londoners rush to escape the city, leaving it abandoned as Ealing, Richmond and Wimbledon are all erased.

The second part of the text returns to the narrator and his hopeless companion, who have now become trapped in a house beside a Martian pit. From this vantage point the narrator is able to witness the Martians at work as captured humans arrive in cages; their blood forms the Martians' staple diet. After two weeks trapped alongside the Martians the curate finally loses his mind and is killed, but the narrator survives and by the time he escapes the Martians have vanished.

So begins the narrator's journey back to the city across a landscape transformed by the disaster. He finally reaches the centre of London, now eerily empty. Drawn by strange cries, he reaches Primrose Hill and witnesses the death of a Martian ravaged by disease. The Martians have succumbed to human bacteria and the nightmare is over. From his vantage point above the city the narrator describes the desolation of dead London, but as the days pass so the people return and finally he heads homeward and is reunited with his wife.

Key London Scene: In the chapter entitled 'Dead London' the narrator returns to the city to find it abandoned and reaching Primrose Hill he looks out over a scene of desolation:

Eastward, over the blackened ruins of the Albert Terrace and the splintered spire of the church, the sun blazed dazzling in a clear sky, and here and there some facet in the great wilderness of roofs caught the light and glared with a white intensity. Northward were Kilburn and Hampstead, blue and crowded with houses; westward the great city was dimmed; and southward, beyond the Martians, the green waves of Regent's Park, the Langham Hotel, the dome of the Albert Hall, the Imperial Institute, and the giant mansions of the Brompton Road came out clear and little in the sunrise, the jagged ruins of Westminster rising hazily beyond. Far away and blue were the Surrey hills, and the towers of the Crystal Palace glittered like two silver rods. The dome of St Paul's was dark against the sunrise, and injured, I saw for the first time, by a huge gaping cavity on its western side.

And as I looked at this wide expanse of houses and factories and churches, silent and abandoned; as I thought of the multitudinous hopes and efforts, the innumerable hosts of lives that had gone to build this human reef, and of the swift and ruthless destruction that had hung over it all; when I realised that the shadow had been rolled back, and that men might still live in the streets, and this dear vast dead city of mine be once more alive and powerful, I felt a wave of emotion that was near akin to tears.

Evaluation: Wells' fantasy is driven by the anxieties of his age. Edwardian fears over unchecked population growth may still be recognised today, but the scenes of mass panic and the resultant brutality of the fleeing populace reflect a view of human nature as being essentially barbarous and requiring firm government control if a collapse into lawlessness is to be prevented.

Most frightening, at least to Wells' middle-class audience, would be the sight of London's safe and homely suburbs as the target for destruction, for it is the cosy familiarity of Woking and Weybridge that makes their annihilation so shocking. The loss of London's East End might to many have appeared more acceptable, even welcome, but Wells seems to revel in his attack on suburbia and to suggest that, in the face of wholesale violence, we all become equally vulnerable. Yet regardless of these attempts to undermine the social structures of his era, Wells' novel ultimately reinforces a view that was to become something of a mantra during the Blitz, that however great the punishment, London can take it, and amid the scenes of desolation Wells remains true to his vision of London as eternal, a city of survivors.

Henry Green, *Caught* (1943)

Author and Background: Henry Vincent Yorke (penname Henry Green) was born in 1905 and educated at Eton and Oxford, where he wrote his first novel, *Blindness* (1926). He later joined the family textile business, but produced a further eight novels, amongst them *Living* (1929), *Party Going* (1939) and *Loving* (1945). His fourth novel, *Caught*, was published in 1943 and was based upon Green's own experiences as a member of the Auxiliary Fire Service during the Blitz. He spent most of his life in London and died in 1973.

Henry Green was heavily influenced by the French writer, Louis-Ferdinand Céline, attempting to describe human behaviour with an equally unflinching honesty. As a result, *Caught* is by no means the straightforward account of wartime heroism that one might expect. While it faithfully records the sacrifice made by these firemen, it does so in a manner that also reveals human weakness, petty divisions and, more surprisingly, a strong underlying sense of sexual opportunism.

Green's wartime novel takes its place alongside other literary recreations of the Blitz, such as Graham Greene's *Ministry of Fear* (1943) and Elizabeth Bowen's *The Heat of the Day* (1948), but unlike these novels and perhaps as a consequence of the time in which it was written, *Caught* stands alone in its unsparing depiction of the city engulfed in flames.

Plot Summary: As the onset of war becomes increasingly inevitable, Richard Roe, a well-to-do widower, joins the Auxiliary Fire Service, returning when his shift ends to his young son Christopher in the countryside. His awkward relationship with his son becomes bound up with his duties to the Fire Service when he finds that his training officer, a man called Pye, is the brother of the disturbed woman who once abducted Christopher and who has been placed in an asylum as a result. In the monotonous days that precede the onset of the Blitz the fire station and its motley assortment of characters become a place of petty disagreements, shifting allegiances and class divisions. An undercurrent of sexual intrigue heightens this uneasy atmosphere, as wartime circumstances momentarily result in an apparent availability of willing women. Gradually, however, the situation deteriorates as Pye, increasingly prone to obscure incestuous memories, begins to behave erratically, thus drawing the attention of his superiors. Following his attempts to help a lost boy, Pye's actions are misinterpreted and he finally commits suicide, but by this stage the bombs have begun to fall and the novel closes with Roe describing the full horrors of the Blitz, which claims the lives of many of the book's characters as London's docks are set ablaze.

Key London Scene: Roe recalls the opening night of the Blitz as he and his crew are sent to the Docks, but he feels unable to convey the immensity of what he has had to face:

As they went, not hurrying, but steadily towards the river, the sky in that quarter, which happened to be the east, beginning at the bottom of streets until it spread over the nearest houses, was flooded in a second sunset, orange and rose, turning the pavements pink. Civilians hastened by twos or threes, hushed below the stupendous pall of defeat until, in the business quarter, the streets were deserted.

These firemen at last drove out on to the bridge. Here two men and a girl, like grey cartridge paper under this light which stretched with the spread of a fan up the vertical sky, were creeping off, drunkenly, defiantly singing.

The firemen saw each other's faces. They saw the water below a dirty yellow towards the fire; the wharves on that far side low and black, those on the bank they were leaving a pretty rose. They saw the whole fury of that conflagration in which they had to play a part. They sat very still, beneath the immensity. For, against it, warehouses, small towers, puny steeples seemed alive with sparks from the mile high pandemonium of flame reflected in the quaking sky. This fan, a roaring red gold, pulsed rose at the outside edge, the perimeter round which the heavens, set with stars before fading into utter blackness, were for a space a trembling green.

Evaluation: As the ambiguity of the title suggests, *Caught* is a novel that undermines conventional notions of wartime heroism by introducing themes of sexual subterfuge, madness and class division as an unexpected backdrop to the destruction of the city. Published in 1943, it is in some ways surprising that the novel was released at all and today it acts as a useful corrective to the official and largely mythological history of the Blitz. Henry Green is by no means a forgotten figure, but *Caught* has not received the attention it deserves in depicting the most significant and most destructive event in London's recent history, a moment that irrevocably altered both the landscape of the city and the mentality of its inhabitants.

JG Ballard, *The Drowned World* (1962)

Author and Background: Born in 1930 in Shanghai, JG Ballard was interned in a civilian prison camp after the attack on Pearl Harbor. He came to England in 1946 and after studying medicine at Cambridge he spent two years with the RAF in Canada. Following the publication of his first novel, *The Wind From Nowhere* in 1962, Ballard became a full-time writer, producing three further disaster novels, *The Drowned World* (1962), *The Drought* (1964) and *The Crystal World* (1965).

Ballard has since written in a number of genres and is now most closely associated with his trilogy of dystopian London novels *Crash* (1973), *Concrete Island* (1974) and *High-Rise* (1975), as well as the autobiographical *Empire of the Sun* (1984). Recent novels include *Cocaine Nights* (1996), *Super-Cannes* (2000) and in a return to London territory, *Millennium People* (2003).

Ballard has been described as the 'Seer of Shepperton' and has created a distinctive imaginative world depicting the suburban realm of motorways and supermarkets that encircles London. Ballard has maintained his belief that it is in the suburbs that the modern world may be most readily identified, in contrast to central London which he regards as buried under the weight of its historical heritage. *The Drowned World* is a novel that takes central London as a setting, but which transforms it into a flooded jungle of the Triassic past. Like so many of his novels, Ballard resists and subverts the conventions of the genre, creating a disaster novel that portrays a post-apocalyptic landscape in a manner startlingly at odds with it predecessors.

Plot Summary: The opening chapter sees the novel's chief protagonist, Robert Kerans, ensconced in a penthouse at the Ritz from where he surveys a city adorned with vast tropical plants and partially submerged within a series of lagoons. Kerans is a member of a biological testing station team sent from their base in the now sub-tropical Arctic Circle to measure the rising temperatures and to survey the flora and fauna in a future London that is fast regressing to its Triassic past. Kerans is accompanied by his commanding officer, Colonel Riggs, and the beautiful but mysterious Doctor Beatrice Dahl. While sampling the luxuries of a bygone era, they note the re-emergence of prehistoric lizards within this extraordinary landscape.

London has become a huge tropical zoo that is subject to stifling heat and yet Kerans and his companions become increasingly reluctant to leave. For soon the characters develop a lethargic passivity, becoming increasingly absorbed by their own primeval dreams, which are triggered by this submerged landscape. Attempts to overcome the reality of this new world give way to a welcoming acceptance of it, as genetic memories of earlier times draw the trio into the surrounding jungle.

This state of aimless passivity is brought to an abrupt end, however, by the arrival of Strangman and his band of modern-day pirates looking to ransack the city for its artistic treasures, and soon Kerans and Strangman are locked in a battle for supremacy over the sunken city. As Strangman begins to drain the lagoons, these equally deranged figures continue their hostilities at street level and Kerans determines to return the lagoons to their submerged state. In the final showdown Kerans sabotages the flood defences, killing Strangman and his crew and injuring himself in the process. As the novel closes, Kerans heads off alone into the jungle in a calculated, but clearly suicidal, attempt to perform some form of psychic reintegration with his evolutionary past.

Key London Scene: Having drained the lagoon, Kerans and Beatrice reach street level and begin to explore what used to be Leicester Square:

> Glancing up uncertainly at the high distant ring of the jungle looming out of the darkness like the encircling lip of an extinct volcanic cone, Kerans led the way across the pavement to the nearest buildings. They stood in the entrance to one of the huge cinemas, sea urchins and cucumbers flickering faintly across the tiled floor, sand dollars flowering in the former ticket booth.
>
> Beatrice gathered her skirt in one hand, and they moved slowly down the lines of cinemas, past cafés and amusement arcades, patronised now only by the bivalves and molluscs. At the first corner they turned away from the sounds of revelry coming from the other side of the square, and walked westwards down the dim dripping canyons. A few star-shells continued to explode overhead, and the delicate glass sponges in the doorways glowed softly as they reflected the pink and blue light.

Evaluation: Many commentators have been bewildered by Ballard's seemingly passive and acquiescent hero and have found his notion of evolutionary regression incoherent, and yet *The Drowned World* is more concerned with imagery than plot. The London that is presented here reveals Ballard's admiration for the Surrealist visions of Ernst, Dali and Delvaux, transposing onto familiar London landmarks the bizarre juxtapositions that characterise these artists' works.

London is portrayed as an evolutionary casualty and its demise is presented without any sense of loss, for these drowned landscapes are depicted as submerged relics of a bygone age. As a consequence, it is fitting that Ballard's novel should be the last example in this cycle of ruined Londons, for this genre has itself since been submerged, having for the moment at least been super-seded by those writers who, like Ballard himself, have chosen to move from the centre to the suburb to explore aspects of the city obscured for rather less dramatic reasons.

Criminal London

'Wordsworth Road,' said my companion. 'Priory Road. Lark Hall Lane. Stockwell Place. Robert Street. Cold Harbour Lane. Our quest does not appear to take us to very fashionable regions.'

Sherlock Holmes, in Sir Arthur Conan Doyle,
The Sign of Four (1890)

The crime novel, at least in the form of the detective story, originates with Edgar Allen Poe's creation MC Auguste Dupin, the detective who solves the case of *The Murders in the Rue Morgue* in 1841. The figure of the detective was soon to leave Paris, however, crossing the Channel and arriving in London, albeit fleetingly, in the work of Charles Dickens both in a number of articles as Inspector Field and later in the novel *Bleak House* (1853) as 'Inspector Bucket of the Detective'.

London had only gained a professional police force of its own following the Metropolitan Police Act of 1829 and for some years after the detection of crime continued to be handled by the Bow Street Runners, a group of prototype private investigators often operating for private reward. But before long, the figure of the detective was widespread within the London novel, appearing in Wilkie Collins' *The Moonstone* (1868) in the guise of Sergeant Cuff. This novel has famously, but wrongly, been described as the first English detective novel, the true pioneer in fact being the now completely forgotten *Notting Hill Mystery* by Charles Felix (1865).

These novels and later Victorian additions to the genre such as Israel Zangwill's *The Big Bow Mystery* (1892) and Arthur Morrison's *Martin Hewitt, Investigator* (1894), are, of course, completely overshadowed by the immortal Sherlock Holmes of Sir Arthur Conan Doyle, who takes his place alongside Dickens and Stevenson in forever defining the Victorian city in the public imagination.

Holmes makes his first appearance in *A Study in Scarlet* (1887) and was soon to return in *The Sign of Four* (1890). Both of these novels, along with numerous short stories, were to develop a figure whose mixture of deductive reasoning and personal peculiarities makes him one of the most recognisable characters in all literature. Yet Conan Doyle's work can be further distinguished from his contemporaries by the way in which London is bound up with the mysteries that Holmes investigates; the city itself is somehow implicated in these crimes and the navigation of its labyrinthine streets is a form of detection in itself. So successful has this model proved to be in delineating the topography of the Victorian city, that the fogbound images of hansom cabs and gas-lit streets continue to resonate with readers more than a century later.

As the detective story moved increasingly from short

story to the novel, new strands emerged within its London form, as the 'penny dreadfuls' of the nineteenth century gave way to pulp fiction such as Sax Rohmer's series of *Fu Manchu* novels that sensationally depicted the 'Yellow Peril' of the East End opium dens, while elsewhere London inspired its own brand of hardboiled *noir* fiction in novels such as Gerald Kersh's *Night and the City* (1938).

Meanwhile, the Golden Age of the crime novel was established through the work of Agatha Christie and Dorothy Sayers, but while their crimes seem to be unvaryingly committed within the confines of a stately home, Margery Allingham provides a rare London-based example in her *The Tiger in the Smoke* (1952), in which a knife-wielding maniac is pursued through the still, fogbound streets of the post-war city.

Eventually, however, after more than half a century, the fog subsided to reveal a city in a more realistic form. Crime soon became less a puzzle to be solved than the depiction of psychological and physical torment amid the harsh realities of the criminal underworld. The darkest of all such imagery was that presented by the writer Robin Cook, whose imaginatively titled satires such as *The Tenants of Dirt Street* (1971) were soon to mutate into the most disturbingly graphic series of crime novels ever written about London. Now writing as Derek Raymond, his 'factory series' portrays a city directly responsible for the shocking plight of both its criminals and their victims, with *I Was Dora Suarez* (1990) being perhaps the bleakest of all.

Today, London *noir* continues to be practised by

writers such as Mark Timlin, in his novels featuring South London private investigator Nick Sharman, while novels such as Anthony Frewin's *London Blues* (1997) and Jake Arnott's *The Long Firm* (1999) reveal the seedy and less-celebrated side of the Swinging Sixties.

All cities have their fictional criminals and all cities have a side usually kept hidden and rarely acknowledged, but London, more than most other cities, encourages, through the disordered and inaccessible layout of its streets, the fictional representation of the crimes that are committed within its boundaries. For these novels themselves only reflect the magnitude of the crimes and criminals that have accumulated here; from Jack Sheppard to Jack the Ripper, from the Richardsons to the Krays, London Crime continues to celebrate its past, for as Iain Sinclair has observed, 'No other strata of society has such a sense of tradition.'

Sir Arthur Conan Doyle, *A Study in Scarlet* (1887)

Author and Background: Sir Arthur Conan Doyle was born in Edinburgh in 1859 and was educated at Stonyhurst and at Edinburgh University, where as a medical student under Professor Joseph Bell he was able to witness the methods that were to provide the model for Holmes' deductive reasoning.

He began to write while working as a doctor in Southsea and Sherlock Holmes first appeared in *A Study in Scarlet* in Beeton's Christmas Annual of 1887. The following that his creation inspired overshadowed the remainder of his life's work, including not only other novels such as *Rodney Stone* (1896) and *The Lost World* (1912), in which his character Professor Challenger was to appear, but also his campaigns for varied political reforms and more than 30 years of inquiry into spiritualism. He died in 1930.

London is the setting and in many ways an active participant in a majority of Holmes' adventures, including his second novel *The Sign of Four* (1889), whose appearance less than a year following the Ripper murders forever cemented a link between the two and granted Holmes an extra-literary existence within the mythology of the Victorian city. Conan Doyle's short story collections, *The Adventures of Sherlock Holmes* (1892) and *The Memoirs of Sherlock Holmes* (1894) further emphasised the city as Holmes' natural habitat, as have numerous films and TV adaptations since. Today, Holmes continues to maintain his position as one of London's leading tourist attractions from his lodgings at 221B Baker Street.

Plot Summary: The narrator, a Dr John H Watson, returning to England to convalesce after military service in Afghanistan, is introduced to Sherlock Holmes and they take lodgings together on Baker Street. Watson is gradually inducted into Holmes' peculiar world, in which his 'science of deduction' is put to use to solve criminal cases in his capacity as a 'consulting detective'. Just as Holmes is complaining about a lack of suitable opportunities to demonstrate his skill, he receives a note informing him of a 'bad business' in Brixton. Soon Holmes and Watson discover a house containing the body of a man called Drebber and the word *Rache* (German for revenge) scrawled in blood upon the wall.

Ignoring the bungling efforts of police Inspector Lestrade, Holmes uses his deductive powers to piece together the mystery and soon he and Watson are chasing across the city in pursuit of the murderer. Luring an associate of the murderer to Baker Street with the help of some street boys in Holmes' service, the man they seek is soon identified as Jefferson Hope, an American working as the driver of a hansom cab. Following the murder of Drebber's secretary, Stangerson, Hope is finally apprehended.

At this point, with the reasoning behind Holmes' success still a mystery, the narrative switches to North America and we learn the background to these strange events: many years before, John Ferrier and his daughter Lucy, abandoned in the desert, are saved by a group of Mormons, amongst them Stangerson and Drebber. Years later, these two men wish to marry Lucy, and when refused they kill both father and daughter. Unknown to them, Lucy is in love with the hunter, Jefferson Hope, who on hearing of her death swears revenge and eventually tracks them down to London. Hope finally admits his guilt, but terminally ill he dies before the case is tried. The novel closes with Holmes outlining the clues and the reasoning that allowed him to solve the crime, while Watson agrees to publish an account of the case.

Key London Scene: Having met for the first time the previous day, and having agreed to become fellow lodgers, Holmes and Watson take a suite of rooms at 221B Baker Street and so establish the most famous fictional address in London:

> We met next day as he had arranged, and inspected the rooms at No. 221B, Baker Street, of which he had spoken at our meeting. They consisted of a couple of comfortable bedrooms and a single large airy sitting-room, cheerfully furnished, and illuminated by two broad windows. So desirable in every way were the apartments, and so moderate the terms seem when divided between us, that the bargain was concluded upon the spot, and we at once entered into possession. That very evening I moved my things round from the hotel, and on the following morning Sherlock Holmes followed me with several boxes and portmanteaux. For a day or two we were busily employed in unpacking and laying out our property to the best advantage. That done, we gradually began to settle down and to accommodate ourselves to our new surroundings.

Evaluation: In an introduction to *A Study in Scarlet*, Iain Sinclair comments: 'It is my contention that certain books overlapping in theme, leave us with characters who achieve an extra-literary existence. Fictional heroes can be real, or more real, than the landscape that contains them. They survive in the general consciousness far longer than the public figures who are their mundane contemporaries.'

This is certainly true of Sherlock Holmes, who resides over London crime fiction as a resident genius and whose celebrity allows him to transcend the fictional confines of those novels in which he appears. He often seems to have outgrown the fictions that produced him and *A Study in Scarlet* only comes alive in those passages in which he is at the forefront. For while Holmes and Watson are a triumphant double act of characterisation, the plot that surrounds them seems rather flimsy by comparison and appears almost too clumsy and awkward to survive their absence. As a result, the American scenes feel faintly ludicrous and it is only once the narrative returns to London that the novel regains its momentum. For Holmes' vitality matches that of the city and seems inseparable from it, and thus when the action is divorced from the streets with which he is so familiar, it is the plot that soon loses its way.

Gerald Kersh, *Night and the City* (1938)

Author and Background: Born in Teddington in 1911, Gerald Kersh began to write at an early age, and while his novel *Jews Without Jehovah* (1934) was the first to find a publisher, it was promptly withdrawn after Kersh was sued by several outraged members of his own family. In a prolific writing career Kersh produced more than 400 short stories and 19 novels, but it was *Night and the City* (1938) that established his reputation. The novel has been filmed twice, with Richard Widmark and more recently Robert De Niro playing the role of Harry Fabian.

During the Second World War, Kersh served with the Coldstream Guards before working as a war correspondent, experiences which were to form the basis for his bestselling book, *They Die With Their Boots Clean* (1941). Kersh spent increasing periods in the USA after the war and was eventually to become an American citizen, but while he continued to write his later years were marked by an increasing dependence upon alcohol. He died in 1968.

Kersh might easily be included here under the category of 'Lost London writing', not least for his novel *Fowler's End* (1957), described by Anthony Burgess as one of the greatest comic novels of the twentieth century. Yet despite its present obscurity, *Night and the City* remains Kersh's finest work and perhaps the greatest example of London *noir*, which for a time between the wars was more than able to compete with its more celebrated American counterparts. Never has London appeared more mean and moody.

Plot Summary: Harry Fabian, an East Ender who presents himself as a successful American songwriter, is in reality a Soho hustler who lives off the earnings of his prostitute girlfriend, Zoe. Beneath the flashy exterior and the grandiose plans, Harry is an amoral chancer and as he moves from club to club amongst his similarly disreputable associates he is always on the lookout for someone to exploit. Such a figure soon emerges in the shape of Arnold Simpson, a lonely and harmless man who visits Zoe for company only to be ruthlessly pursued by Harry, who, having tracked him down to his home, proceeds to blackmail him. A hundred pounds richer, Harry decides to reinvent himself as a wrestling promoter and has soon gone into partnership in Fabian Promotions. Naturally though, Harry has soon blown his money in a Soho nightclub and it is here that his story becomes intertwined with that of Helen, a new hostess with dreams of wealth, and her lover Adam, an aspiring sculptor working as a waiter.

Gradually Harry's life begins to disintegrate as he gambles away his money, loses his business, and through his infatuation with Helen loses his girlfriend and provider, Zoe. Meanwhile, we witness Helen's corruption as she is lured deeper into the underworld by the promise of riches, while only Adam escapes unscathed, turning his back on a life of cheap squalor to pursue his artistic dreams. As the novel ends, Harry is broke, pursued by enemies, and is finally arrested as Zoe turns him in to the police.

Key London Scene: As the evening descends the bars and the clubs of the West End begin to fill and Harry's night-time city comes alive:

Ping! went the clock, on the first stroke of eight. Up and down the streets the shops began to close. West Central started to flare and squirm in a blazing vein-work of neon-tubes. Bursting like inexhaustible fireworks, the million coloured bulbs of the electric signs blazed in a perpetual recurrence over the face of the West End. Underground trains from the suburbs squirting out of their tunnels like red toothpaste out of tubes disgorged theatre-crowds. Loaded buses rumbled towards the dog-tracks. Cinema vestibules became black with people. Vaudeville theatres, like gigantic vacuum-cleaners, suddenly sucked in waiting queues. Behind upper windows lights clicked on and blinds snapped down. Gas, wire, wax, oil – everything burned that would give out light. The darkness of the April night got thicker. It seeped down between the street lamps, poured into basements, and lay deep and stagnant under the porches and the arches of the back streets. The last of the shop doors slammed. The places where one could eat, drink, and amuse oneself remained open, and burned with a lurid and smoky brightness. Night closed down upon the city.

Evaluation: Kersh's novel may be set in the 1930s, but his observations of human weakness and despair retain a timeless quality. Similarly, his depictions of the everyday struggle to survive within an unforgiving city are equally pertinent today, when the lure of wealth and success and its by-products of corruption and misery are as visible as ever. The London Kersh portrays is one of contrasts, and while the moral divisions between strength and weakness, honesty and deception may seem a little forced at times, as is his use of wrestling to allegorise this struggle, Kersh is unerring in his eye for the amorality of the night-time city where only money holds any meaning.

Margery Allingham, *The Tiger in the Smoke* (1952)

Author and Background: Born in 1904, Margery Allingham belongs to the 'Golden Age' of the detective story that flourished between the wars, although it was her later novels that proved most successful. Like Agatha Christie's Poirot and Dorothy Sayers' Lord Peter Wimsey, Allingham was responsible for the creation of one of the finest fictional sleuths. Albert Campion is perhaps the greatest London detective since Sherlock Holmes and like his illustrious predecessor tends to overshadow the plot of many of Allingham's novels. Yet in later books such as *More Work for the Undertaker* (1948) and *Tiger in the Smoke* (1952), Campion takes on a lesser role as the city itself comes to the forefront of the story. The latter novel, which is unquestionably her finest, evokes a powerful sense of the post-war city as a place of violence and fear hidden beneath the ubiquitous fog. In placing Campion very much in the margins while turning the spotlight firmly on the novel's psychopathic anti-hero, Allingham moves a long way from the country house murders of the 20s and 30s. Margery Allingham died in 1966.

Plot Summary: Geoffrey Levett and Meg Elginbrodde are engaged to be married, but Meg has begun to receive letters and photos from a man claiming to be her first husband, who had been presumed missing in action. Albert Campion and Chief Inspector Luke, suspecting blackmail, become involved in the case and soon apprehend the impostor. But clearly too terrified to talk, the suspect is released only to be promptly murdered, while Levett, who is himself investigating the case, then vanishes. Soon it becomes clear that recent jail-breaker Jack Havoc is on the rampage and, having killed the suspect along with several other men, a manhunt begins across the city. Havoc, it turns out, was a wartime comrade of Meg's first husband Martin and along with a crew of ex-military men and assorted misfits is now hunting Meg, whom he believes knows the whereabouts of hidden treasure. These men have captured Levett, who is eventually released by Campion, but the knife-wielding maniac manages to escape to France, where, having located the treasure, he is finally cornered and throws himself to his death.

Key London Scene: The novel opens with a depiction of the city shrouded in yellow fog and the city remains obscured throughout, the fog only lifting when the case itself has been cleared-up:

"It may be only blackmail," said the man in the taxi hopefully. The fog was like a saffron blanket soaked in ice water. It had hung over London all day and at last was beginning to descend. The sky was yellow as a duster and the rest was a granular black, over-printed in grey and lightened by occasional slivers of bright fish colour as a policeman turned in his wet cape.

Already the traffic was at an irritable crawl. By dusk it would be stationary. To the west the Park dripped wretchedly and to the north the great railway terminus slammed and banged and exploded hollowly about its affairs. Between lay winding miles of butter-coloured stucco in every conceivable state of repair.

The fog had crept into the taxi where it crouched panting in a traffic jam. It oozed in ungenially, to smear sooty fingers over the two elegant young people who sat inside. They were keeping apart self-consciously, each stealing occasional glances in the same kind of fear at their clasped hands resting between them on the shabby leather seat.

Evaluation: Before the novel opens Allingham notes, 'In the shady ways of Britain today it is customary to refer to the Metropolis of London as the Smoke.' This rather formal tone may often seem dated to the contemporary reader. Similarly, Campion himself often comes across as a bumbling upper-class caricature more at home in a PG Wodehouse novel, and while largely redundant here, he is a continued reminder of a bygone age. Yet beneath this rather dated style, *The Tiger in the Smoke* accurately reveals the deprivation and violence of the post-war city, in which its population of newly demobbed soldiers often found it difficult to adapt to civilian life, instead putting their military training to criminal ends. Jack Havoc is a surprisingly disturbing figure, his bizarre psychopathic 'philosophy' very much at odds with the detective fiction of the pre-war years and he rightly takes his place within the pantheon of London's fictional killers.

Derek Raymond, *I Was Dora Suarez* (1990)

Author and Background: Born in London in 1931, Robin Cook was educated at Eton until he was 16, when he walked out. Military service and work in the family textile business followed, but finding neither to his liking, Cook began a prolonged period of residence abroad in the USA, Europe and North Africa. He turned to writing in the 1960s and his novel, *The Crust on Its Uppers* (1962), was the first in a series of satirical observations of London's lowlife, culminating in *The Tenants of Dirt Street* (1971). This marks the first chapter of Cook's life and after a long absence from writing, during which time he moved to France, Cook re-emerged in the mid-eighties under the pseudonym Derek Raymond and began his series of 'Factory' novels, some of the darkest and bleakest depictions of London's underworld ever written. These began with *The Devil's Home on Leave* (1985) and reached their high (or low) point with *I Was Dora Suarez* (1990), certainly his most disturbing book. Raymond described himself as a practitioner of the 'Black Novel' and his contribution to London *noir* is a departure from anything that preceded it, offering an intensity and unflinching vision that has little in common with earlier accounts of the city and its criminal underclass. Since his death in 1994, Raymond has continued to influence London writers from Mark Timlin to Iain Sinclair and Chris Petit, whose London novel *Robinson* (1993) contains in the character Cookie a fictional portrayal of Raymond.

Plot Summary: Dora Suarez, a 30-year-old prostitute, and Betty Carstairs, an 86-year-old widow, are discovered murdered and horribly disfigured in their London flat. Later the same evening a nightclub owner and racketeer has his head blown off. These apparently unrelated killings are assigned to Raymond's unnamed Detective Sergeant, who, along with his colleague Stevenson, set out to find the killer. Soon it becomes clear that the murders are the work of the same man, a psychopathic killer with a long history of grotesque killings, and gradually our unnamed detective becomes obsessed with the case and with the tragic history of Dora Suarez, which is revealed in her diary.

Dora's diary makes for depressing reading, outlining as it does her degrading life as a prostitute and her gradual decline to the ravages of AIDS. It turns out that she was planning on taking her own life before the killer did the job for her and soon the detectives are investigating the nightclub in which she once worked. Here they discover the true horrors of her existence and pick up the trail of the killer, an Italian doorman with bizarre sado-masochistic tendencies who lives in an abandoned warehouse. The novel closes as the detectives corner him, and having decided that he must die for his crimes, the Detective Sergeant executes him with his own gun.

Key London Scene: The killer's victims live in one of those faceless apartment blocks that are so common in London, where amidst a crowded residential area people live lives of isolation and neglect. In this environment a murderer can operate unmolested:

Now he felt like inching back in a rat-like posture, bold but careful, to the spot by the window where he had left his shoulder-bag and listened, but there wasn't a sound to be heard in the flats as he got a rag out of the old Adidas hold-all and began to wipe his axe, taking care not to cut himself – Christ it was sharp! As for the silence in the flats, that didn't surprise him at all, for they stood in a prime residential area where the big property combines had forgotten very few places indeed and catered for the old and rich, who didn't care what rent and rates they paid as long as, in return, they didn't have to be pestered over the unemployed, ethnic minorities, handicapped people or anything else even remotely disturbing. It was, as a matter of fact, because the tenants of Empire Gate didn't want to know about anything unpleasant at all that enabled the killer to behave more or less as if he were at home.

Evaluation: I Was Dora Suarez is quite unlike any other London novel and appears to have very little in common with the fictions of Kersh or Allingham. The detection of the crime is subordinated to an examination of the psychological states of the principal characters and this London is populated only by victims and their tormentors. Raymond has his imitators, but remains alone in describing a city completely without warmth or glamour in which evil is less the exception than the norm and in which horrific episodes go unnoticed or ignored. What earlier novelists in this tradition only hint at Raymond makes shockingly graphic, his vision one of a city that in wilfully over-looking the plight of its inhabitants is itself implicated in the crimes that are committed behind its bland façades.

Anthony Frewin, *London Blues* (1997)

Author and Background: Born in London, Anthony Frewin spent more than 20 years in the film business as Assistant Director and PA to Stanley Kubrick. Having written non-fiction books on both film and on the Kennedy assassination, Frewin turned to fiction in 1997 with his novel *London Blues*, which was followed by *Sixty-Three Closure* (1998) and *Scorpion Rising* (1999). These novels are very much self-consciously written within the *noir* tradition, and *London Blues*, which has been described as the 'quintessential Soho book' recreates the London of the early sixties, marrying true events and characters with a fictional account of the seedier side of the Swinging Sixties. Soho, of course, has its own tradition as the site of London fiction and Frewin's debut novel has much in common with other, more recent, Soho fictions, notably Chris Petit's *Robinson* (1990), which similarly explores London's underground film community, and Jake Arnott's *The Long Firm* (1999), which also returns to the sixties and a time when London was re-emerging as the cultural capital of the world. *London Blues* focuses not only on Soho, however, but also provides a rare fictional excursion into the resolutely downmarket streets of Bayswater and Queensway, revealing those same faceless areas and marginal lives documented by Derek Raymond.

Plot Summary: Tim Purdom moves from Rochester in Kent to London at the start of the sixties. He soon acquires a job in a Soho café and dingy rooms in Bayswater, then begins to explore the city and its seedy charms. His work in Soho allows him to discover a more profitable sideline in shooting porn films and gradually he becomes a figure in the secretive world of the Soho porn scene. As Soho changes in the early sixties and cafés give way to sex shops, so Purdom's career takes off as he becomes involved in filming 'parties' for many of the establishment figures of the day. The narrative becomes increasingly interwoven with the political events and personalities of this period and through his acquaintance with Dr Stephen Ward, Purdom is caught up in the conspiracies surrounding the Profumo Affair. Too late he realises that he is out of his depth and involved in a dangerous circle that has manipulated him and his role as filmmaker. Set up in a drugs bust, he is arrested, his flat searched and, followed and monitored by unknown persons, he is eventually caught up in the murders of his friends. He escapes and survives to witness the downfall of the Conservative government in 1964, but as Wilson's Labour government takes power his flat and, it would appear, he himself are destroyed in an explosion. The novel ends with as many questions as answers, and his role in the political machinations surrounding him remains unclear. Years later he is spotted in his hometown of Rochester. Is he really dead?

Key London Scene: Tim's childhood friend George, who narrates much of the story, returns to London many years after these events and recalls the Bayswater of the 1960s, a time and a place now part of 'Lost London':

To the south is the Bayswater Road and that part of Hyde Park that dissolves into Kensington Gardens, while to the north is Westbourne Grove where I now head. Up past the old Whiteley's department store on the left, now revamped as some co-operative boutique collective with flags flying at high mast above it, and then across the Grove.

I continue, in an easterly direction, past the road that leads up to the Porchester Baths, past the old ABC Cinema.

I turn left on to Porchester Road and stop. I'm standing outside the Royal Oak pub, a place that looks like it must have been here for a hundred years or more. It's a pub with more local than passing trade I would guess, an unprepossessing place that probably hasn't changed since the war and one that won't until the day a developer gets planning permission to demolish and redevelop, then it'll become part of what it already seems – another part of Lost London.

And there's Timmy drinking at the bar, just in there, only a few yards away from me… but nearly thirty years ago. He's part of Lost London too, the Valhalla of Memory. All the parameters are right except for that of Time. We could have met. Yes, indeed.

I turn my head slowly. I know what to expect

from sly peripheral vision glances. What was there is no longer there. I'm dealing in the vanished. The stuff of memories. The London that is gone.

Evaluation: 'This is a lost mystery of Lost London' says the narrator, and *London Blues* is very much a meditation upon time and the passing of an era into myth and memory. Frewin skilfully interweaves fact and fiction in recreating a period in London's past that can no longer be separated from the myths that it has accumulated, a time when the city was undergoing enormous change and in which both people and places soon found themselves becoming obsolete. Frewin accurately evokes the paranoia of political intrigue and conspiracy theory, in which once again the veneer of establishment life is exposed as concealing something much less respectable and London itself is shown to lead a double life in which nothing is as it appears.

Lost London Writing

'But it's not just the streets that can be banished into the theatre of memory; books and the people who write them are doomed to go the same way. If fame is oblivion postponed, there is also the privileged anonymity of the antiquarian bookdealer's catalogue. A poignant fate in which a book's value (its purchase price) climbs vertiginously in relation to its occulted status.'

Iain Sinclair, 'Excavating the Unburied:
Some London Writers' in *Waterstone's Guide
to London Writing* (1999)

Iain Sinclair has written at some length about those London writers he describes as the 'reforgotten' – authors who have slipped from memory and whose neglected titles form an alternative canon of the overlooked. For many London writers are fêted in their own day only to disappear quickly from view, occasionally resurfacing belatedly to receive their rightful recognition, more often returning to languish once again in out-of-print obscurity.

Thus while Dickens remains unassailable in his dominance of the Victorian literary landscape, his celebrated contemporaries GWM Reynolds and William Pett

Ridge have since sunk without trace. Similarly, while the bright young things of Mayfair and Bloomsbury remain forever immortalised in Virginia Woolf's *Mrs Dalloway* (1925) and Evelyn Waugh's *Vile Bodies* (1930), the London of spivs and petty criminals recreated in the fiction of James Curtis now seems lost forever, while Robert Westerby's novel, *Wide Boys Never Work* (1937), which deserves to be remembered for its title alone, is sadly not remembered at all. As a consequence, the London of this period is unevenly depicted by fiction that is in its narrow, class-bound perspective hardly representative of the wider city and it is left to writers such as Patrick Hamilton in his *Hangover Square* (1941) to maintain the memory of London's seedier side.

Wartime London inspired a wealth of fictional recreations, but as with all novels that are born out of a particular historical moment, however momentous, they run the risk of failing to survive that moment's passing. While Graham Greene's *The End of the Affair* (1951) and, to a lesser extent, Henry Green's *Caught* (1943) appear to have survived the test of time, Elizabeth Bowen's *The Heat of the Day* (1948), has become increasingly unfashionable despite remaining the truest evocation of the dislocation and pervasive unreality of the London of this time.

Elsewhere, writing may come to mirror the fate of the community that produced it, and while the Jewish tradition of London writing has been surprisingly prolific its current neglect is reflected in its accounts of a way of life, especially in the old East End, that was soon to vanish forever. Two such writers are particularly worthy of mention here: Gerald Kersh has already appeared in the chapter on London crime with his novel *Night and the City* (1938), but both for this and for his later comic account of the grotesque London suburb *Fowler's End* (1957) Kersh would warrant entry here, and the same is true of Alexander Baron, whose novel, *The Lowlife* (1963), still inspires a cult following but is otherwise forgotten.

In a similar fashion, London novels may fall victim to their own success in capturing a moment of transition that once recorded is almost immediately overtaken by the events that they anticipate. Hence Colin MacInnes' *Absolute Beginners* (1959) may have been the first to record the youthful unrest of the late fifties, but it has not aged well and now reads as little more than a period piece, while Sam Selvon's account of the experiences of the early Caribbean immigrants to the city, *The Lonely Londoners* (1956) in capturing an authentic cadence of tone, has perhaps distanced itself from a wider readership.

Yet looking for the reasons why such novels are met with continued support or with sustained indifference is ultimately futile, for some of the finest London writers simply don't receive their due. Maureen Duffy's wonderful *Capital* (1975) is a case in point, having garnered little of the acclaim it deserves.

In the end, all London writing is bound to record an image of Lost London and is inevitably involved in an act of commemoration for the city's past. Today, perhaps more than ever before, in an environment in which these links are eroded and the past is increasingly sacrificed or repackaged, these lost London writers may be resurrected to remind us that the act of remembrance has never been so necessary.

Patrick Hamilton, *Hangover Square* (1941)

Author and Background: Born in Sussex in 1904 and educated at Westminster, Patrick Hamilton's first novel, *Monday Morning*, was published in 1925. It was followed by the play *Rope* (1929), later to be filmed by Hitchcock, and the novels *The Midnight Bell* (1929), *The Siege of Pleasure* (1932) and *The Plains of Cement* (1934), which together form the trilogy of London novels, *Twenty Thousand Streets Under the Sky* (1935). His masterpiece, *Hangover Square*, was published in 1941 and despite increasing problems with alcoholism, Hamilton became one of the most celebrated novelists of his day, continuing to write until his death in 1962.

Hangover Square, subtitled '*A Story of Darkest Earl's Court*', is one of the great London novels and neither the novel nor its creator can accurately be described as 'lost'. Such a term is more than suitable, however, for the book's characters, a group of idle, shiftless boozers who aimlessly move from bar to bar, and in George Harvey Bone, Hamilton created a character whose moving combination of innocence, naivety, and vulnerability symbolised the loneliness and despair of all those isolated figures that the city has treated so harshly.

Plot Summary: George Harvey Bone leads a solitary existence in an Earl's Court Hotel from where he strolls each day to a series of seedy pubs. His life is completely aimless until the moment when something 'clicks' inside his head and he is transported to a grey and unfeeling world where he discovers his true purpose – to kill Netta Longdon, the women he loves.

George is infatuated by Netta and his life revolves around her every movement. Unfortunately for him, however, Netta does not reciprocate these feelings for she is a callous, evil woman who delights in manipulating and tormenting George while spending all his money. She is joined in this pursuit by her circle of equally repellent friends, amongst them her occasional lover, the fascist Peter. Together they drift from bar to bar, from London to Brighton, making George's life a series of ever more painful humiliations and while George is partially aware of this situation he is unable to escape from Netta's spell. It is only in his schizophrenic 'dead' moods that he clearly sees the reality of their relationship and realises without emotion that he must kill both her and Peter.

A chance meeting with an old school friend seems to offer George an escape route from his nightmarish existence, but every time it looks as if he will free himself from his obsession, he is lured back by Netta's cunning insinuations. Finally, just when it appears that he has finally broken away for good, he hears the familiar click in his head and, returning to Earl's Court, he calmly dispatches Netta and Peter before making his way to Maidenhead, where, faced with the hopelessness of his situation, he takes his own life.

Key London Scene: Returning to London from Brighton by train, George approaches the city with increasing trepidation, realising that it is the site of his greatest fears:

> The wheels and track clicked out the familiar and unmistakeable rhythm – the sly, gentle suggestive rhythm, unlike any of its others, of a train entering a major London terminus, and he was filled with unease and foreboding as he always was by this sound. Thought and warmth must give place to action in cold streets – reality, buses, tubes, booking-offices, life again, electric-lit London, endless terrors.
>
> Oh dear! – here we were – here was the platform under the huge roof – hollow, hellish echoing noises as in a swimming bath, and the porters lined up for the attack – no getting out of it now! Foreboding gave place almost to panic. Liverpool Street. Where was he going? What was his plan of campaign? He realised he had made none...

Evaluation: This is the archetypal novel of thirties London – the fog, smoke, booze, bars and boarding houses all overshadowed by premonitions of the forth-coming war. It's all presented completely without glamour as we witness the pathetic drunken descent into inevitable madness and despair. And in tandem with this individual tragedy we also glimpse the begin-nings of a wider and equally predictable tragedy unfolding in the newspapers as war is declared. For Hamilton, the inevitable suffering of individual life is mirrored both across an unfeeling city and across an equally unfeeling world, yet this message is delivered with both compassion and the blackest humour and one never loses sympathy for George's plight.

Elizabeth Bowen, *The Heat of the Day* (1948)

Author and Background: Elizabeth Bowen was born in Dublin in 1899 and educated in Kent. She married in 1923 and travelled a great deal, dividing her time between London and her family home in County Cork, the subject of her family history, *Bowen's Court* (1942). Her first book, *Encounters*, a collection of short stories, was published in 1923 and was followed by a series of novels including *The Hotel* (1927), *The Last September* (1929), *To the North* (1932), *The House in Paris* (1935), *The Death of the Heart* (1938) and *The Heat of the Day* (1948). Her last book, *Eva Trout*, was published in 1969. She died in 1973.

During her lifetime Bowen was regarded as a major novelist and was awarded a CBE in 1948, yet despite this widespread acclaim her reputation has somewhat diminished since her death and her books have fallen out of fashion. Her work bridges the Irish literary tradition and the English avant-garde and her finest novels, *The Death of the Heart* and *The Heat of the Day*, evoke a powerful sense of place both in Ireland and London. These novels both begin in the setting of Regent's Park, Bowens' home during the war years until bombed out in 1944, and in *The Heat of the Day* Bowen captures both the heightened intensity, as well as the new-found intimacy that characterised the lives of Londoners during the war. Like Woolf before her, Bowen rarely strays from the confines of upper-class life and yet within these admittedly narrow boundaries she successfully portrays a city haunted by the ghosts of the unknown dead.

Plot Summary: Set in the summer of 1942, *The Heat of the Day* tells the story of Stella Rodney, a widow living in a rented flat in Mayfair, and explores her relationship with her son, Roderick, who has just joined the Army, and her lover, Robert, a Dunkirk invalid now working in Intelligence. Stella's ordered existence is disrupted by the intrusion of Harrison, a man she first meets at a funeral in Ireland. Harrison is an anonymous figure whose motives remain obscure, but having forced his way into Stella's world he informs her that her lover is in fact a traitor and that he is in a position to expose him. He warns Stella that if she tells Robert of his claims then he will be immediately unmasked, an event that is likely to prove fatal. However, he insinuates that such a fate can be avoided if Stella becomes his lover or companion. As the novel progresses, switching in intervals between wartime London and Roderick's newly inherited home in Ireland, Stella maintains her silence but continues to frustrate Harrison until finally she confronts Robert with the truth. Robert eventually admits to his guilt and believing himself to be cornered falls or leaps from Stella's roof and is killed. The novel closes as Stella attempts to rebuild her life and as the war turns in the Allies' favour London prepares for the invasion of Europe.

Key London Scene: The autumn of 1940 saw the first air raids and with it came both the fear of imminent death and an awareness of the city as a living entity:

Never had any season been more felt; one bought the poetic sense of it with the sense of death. Out of mists of morning charred by the smoke from ruins each day rose to a height of unmisty glitter; between the last of sunset and first note of the siren the darkening glassy tenseness of evening was drawn fine. From the moment of waking you tasted the sweet autumn not less because of an acridity on the tongue and nostrils; and as the singed dust settled and smoke diluted you felt more and more called upon to observe the daytime as a curious holiday from fear. All through London, the ropings-off of dangerous tracts of street made islands of exalted if stricken silence, and people crowded against the ropes to admire the sunny emptiness on the other side. The diversion of traffic out of blocked main thoroughfares into byways, the unstopping phantasmagoric streaming of lorries, buses, vans, drays, taxis past modest windows and quiet doorways set up an overpowering sense of London's organic power – somewhere here was a source from which heavy motion boiled, surged, and, not to be damned up, forced for itself new channels.

Evaluation: Written in 1948, *The Heat of the Day* looks back on the war years with a mixture of nostalgia and regret. For despite the long nights of fear and the prevailing sense of loss, the early years of the war were marked by an intensity never to be repeated. London is presented as a strangely empty city, manned only by the 'garrison society' that has chosen to remain and amongst these Londoners a curious freedom builds as barriers between people gradually dissolve. Bowen captures the pervasive unreality of this situation, in which an untimely death was a very real possibility and examines the sense of dislocation provoked by the absence of familiar buildings and their inhabitants. Together with Henry Green's *Caught, The Heat of the Day* provides a powerful portrait of a threatened city and its inhabitants.

Samuel Selvon, *The Lonely Londoners* (1956)

Author and Background: Samuel Selvon was born in 1923 in Trinidad to Indian parents and began his writing career as a local journalist. Having served in the West Indian Navy during the war, Selvon produced a number of short stories before moving to England where he published his first novel, *A Brighter Sun*, in 1952. Several novels were to follow, amongst them *An Island Is a World* (1955), *Ways of Sunlight* (1957) and *I Hear Thunder* (1963). Many of these works were chiefly concerned with life in his native Trinidad, but it was with his account of the early Caribbean experience in London, *The Lonely Londoners* (1956), that he first received widespread acclaim. Selvon was to write two further novels featuring the novel's hero, Moses Aloetta, *Moses Ascending* (1975) and *Moses Migrating* (1983), in which Moses returns to Trinidad. Selvon himself left London in 1978, moving to Calgary in Canada. He died during a visit to Trinidad in 1994.

Selvon received some critical acknowledgement during his lifetime and was granted an Honorary Doctorate by Warwick University in 1989 and yet his work has since been largely neglected. *The Lonely Londoners* deserves a wider readership, for with its pioneering use of Trinidadian dialect and sharp eye for the fast-changing landscape of 1950s London the novel remains the most expressive account we have of immigrant life in the post-war city.

Plot Summary: As the novel opens Moses Aloetta is going to Waterloo to meet a new arrival from Trinidad. Moses has been in London for almost ten years and acts as something of a mentor to those just arriving from his homeland, helping them to find accommodation, work and community.

Henry Oliver, subsequently known as Sir Galahad, arrives in a summer suit and with no belongings, and while he talks bravely of his big plans he soon realises that he cannot survive without Moses' support. Galahad is the first in the series of larger than life characters that people the novel and whose adventures form the bulk of the text.

The Captain, an effortless charmer never short of a girlfriend, Tolroy, broke and supporting a large extended family, Big City, a hustler always on the make, and Five Past Twelve, always borrowing money and looking for a party; these characters lead an eventful life of hardship and excitement bound within the streets of Bayswater and Westbourne Grove. This is a London dominated by cheap boarding houses in the winter and Hyde Park in the summer, and in the centre of it all is Moses, dispensing advice and support to all but still torn between the familiarity of his new home and his memories of Trinidad.

Key London Scene: Despite loneliness, discomfort and prejudice, Selvon wonders what it is about the city that still attracts people to it and then prevents them from leaving:

The changing of the seasons, the cold slicing winds, the falling leaves, sunlight on green grass, snow on the land, London particular. Oh what it is and where it is and why it is, no one knows, but to have said: 'I walked on Waterloo Bridge,' 'I rendezvoused at Charing Cross,' 'Piccadilly Circus is my playground,' to say these things, to have lived these things, to have lived in the great city of London, centre of the world. To one day lean against the wind walking up the Bayswater Road (destination unknown), to see the leaves swirl and dance and spin on the pavement (sight unseeing), to write a casual letter home beginning: 'Last night, in Trafalgar Square...'

What it is that a city have, that any place in the world have, that you get so much to like it you wouldn't leave it for anywhere else? What it is that would keep men although by and large, in truth and in fact, they catching their royal to make a living,

125

staying in a cramp-up room where you have to do everything – sleep, eat, dress, wash, cook, live. Why it is, that although they grumble about it all the time, curse the people, curse the government, say all kind of thing about this and that, why it is, that in the end, everyone cagey about saying outright that if the chance come they will go back to them green islands in the sun?

Evaluation: Selvon's account of the Caribbean immigrant community in West London continues a tradition begun with Jean Rhys' tale of a young Caribbean girl arriving in London, *Voyage in the Dark* (1934) and was highly influential on writers such as Colin MacInnes, whose *Absolute Beginners* (1959) covers a similar territory. But while MacInnes' prose now reads as painfully dated, Selvon's novel retains an authenticity and immediacy that balances the excitement of the times with a wistful acknowledgement of what has been left behind. In a deceptively simple manner, *The Lonely Londoners* depicts a city which, despite its austerity and indifference, can still enthral those experiencing it for the first time.

Alexander Baron, *The Lowlife* (1963)

Author and Background: Alexander Baron was born in 1917 in Hackney, East London, where he was educated and spent most of his life. He became involved at an early age with the struggle against Fascism, and with Moseley's Blackshirts increasingly prominent in the East End he left school to work for the youth wing of the Communist Party. After active service in the Army during the war, Baron wrote his first novel, *From the City, From the Plough* in 1948. Based on his wartime experiences, it was a great success and allowed him to write full-time. He was to become a prolific writer, producing 14 novels mostly set in London, including *The Lowlife* (1963) and *King Dido* (1969), as well as writing several television screenplays. Yet despite his early success, Baron's reputation soon waned and apart from the cult following that *The Lowlife* still commands, his work is now largely neglected.

Plot Summary: Harryboy Boas, gambler and Zola enthusiast, lives in an anonymous Hackney boarding house. His life revolves around the bookies and the dog-track and occasional visits to the West End to visit Marcia who charges him twenty pounds for the privilege. When short of money he works as an occasional Hoffman presser in a factory and when on a winning streak he spends his days in bed reading. His sister Debbie lives in upmarket Finchley where her husband regards Harryboy with disdain and otherwise he leads a solitary existence.

Into this carefully ordered world come the Deaners, a family who move in downstairs and soon their child Gregory has entered his life. Gradually Harryboy forms a relationship with this family, his outwardly flashy existence soon leading Gregory's father Vic to try his hand, unsuccessfully, as a gambler and as he gets into trouble Harry vows to help. But soon Harry has troubles of his own, for having endured a long losing streak he takes on work as a rent-collector for Marcia, but when he blows the money he has collected for her he is soon pursued by her hired heavies. His situation deteriorates and having turned to his sister for help, he falls out with his brother-in-law. In the final showdown, he manages to avoid a beating, and as his luck turns he is able to settle his debts. As the novel closes, however, the boy Gregory blinds himself with a firework and, wanting to make a heroic gesture, Harry offers his own eye for transplant. But in Harry's world even this gesture falls flat, and with the boy finding another donor, Harry is left much as he started, broke and alone.

Key London Scene: When Harry has any money he heads west towards the bars and the restaurants, yet while he aspires to a wealthy lifestyle and has grandiose plans of being a property owner, he knows that Hackney is his true home and is unable to escape from its familiar streets:

Fellows ask me, especially when my wallet is full, why I should live in Hackney. Why not? – that's enough to answer.

Still, there is more to it. A lot of gambling fellows live in the West End, near the whores and the restaurants. Me? I want to live where I grew up. God knows, there's no one left – hardly anyone, a face here and there – but that's why the place holds me. There's only the place left.

Also, I like it. Here it is, a Victorian-Edwardian suburb swallowed up by London, broad streets, little

MERLIN COVERLEY

villas and big tradesman's houses; and now, among
these, factories and workshops everywhere, little
workshops in the mews, big yellow-brick factories
on the corner sites. Traffic roars in the streets. Here,
all sorts live. The Cockneys are of the old breed,
sharp-faced, with the stamp of the markets on them.
The young Jews either look like pop singers or pop
singers' managers. The old ones – it's funny, the pious
old men with yellow beards I remember from my
childhood seem to have died off, but the old women
survive. Among the crowds you can see the old
women, women you might have seen in the east end
fifty years ago (Hackney isn't the East End – that's
the mark of the outsider, when you hear someone
call Hackney the East End. The East End starts two
miles down the road, across the border of Bethnal
Green) schlepping their big shopping bags.

Evaluation: The Lowlife is a faithful evocation of Lost
London by a Lost London writer. The Hackney that
Baron describes has all but vanished since the sixties;
the Victorian terraces destroyed and replaced with
tower blocks or else gentrified and bought up by those
working in the nearby City. Similarly, the Jewish
community has largely moved elsewhere, to be replaced
by a new cycle of immigrants as the book indicates. The
London portrayed here seems an insular community
stranded from the rest of the city and known only to
the locals who have been brought up here, with none
of the fashionable status it has acquired today. Hackney
is for Baron a world within a world and he successfull

brings to life an area that is more often portrayed simply as a symbol for London's ills.

Maureen Duffy, *Capital* (1975)

Author and Background: Born in Worthing in 1933, Maureen Duffy spent her childhood on the South Coast and in the East End of London. She published her first poem at the age of 17 and, having studied at King's College London, became a schoolteacher in London before becoming a full-time writer. She has since produced a stream of plays and novels, as well as works of biography, history and literary criticism. Amongst these are her trilogy of London novels, *Wounds* (1969), *Capital* (1975) and *Londoners* (1983) and most recently *Alchemy* (2004).

Her inclusion here rests upon her novel *Capital*, one of the strangest and greatest of all London fictions. Needless to say, the majority of Duffy's work has been largely overlooked and like so many of the books listed here, its neglect mirrors the lives of those marginalised characters the novel celebrates, these unrecorded lives forming the unwritten history of the city.

Plot Summary: Meepers, amateur archaeologist and eccentric loner, lives in a garden shed in a London square. He is obsessed by the history of the city and in particular by the Dark Ages, when London was said to have been destroyed. He hopes through his research to disprove this theory and by establishing an unbroken history that precedes the Dark Ages he can demonstrate not only London's ability to survive past calamities, but also to survive an uncertain future. Meepers has a job as a porter at a London University college and here he comes into contact with Emery, a historian who once rejected one of his papers. These two lonely individuals form an unlikely friendship and through their shared interest in the past they begin to overcome the problems of their present.

This story is itself interspersed with episodes from London history, from the earliest Neanderthal inhabitants, through the Norman invasion, the Black Death and Peasants' Revolt to the Blitz and the contemporary city. Meepers is haunted by the voices of these earlier Londoners who guide him on his expeditions across the city. Yet modern London is a hostile place that denies Meepers a home and he is forced to move from place to place, eventually finding his way to a tower block in the centre of the city. From here he entertains those friends that his studies have introduced him to, but he has become a ghost himself, an increasingly invisible figure whose death at the end of the novel releases him to join the inhabitants of the dead city that have so intrigued him.

Key London Scene: The novel begins with Meepers walking through the streets aware of all those buried Londoners whose bones lie beneath his feet:

He couldn't help it if the bones poked through the pavements under his feet; plague victims, there was a pit hereabouts he was sure, jumbled together, massacred Danes weighted by their axes to the river-bed, the cinders of legionaries in porphyry and glass urns gritting beneath the soles of his thin shoes. It was the living who passed ghostly around him, through whose curiously incorporeal flesh he moved without sensation while the dead pressed and clamoured, their cries drowning out the traffic. As he passed below, long buried noblemen looked down at him from the portrait gallery of street names enshrining their riverside mansions and estates above his head. Well he had kept his while most of them had lost theirs, one way or the other. He looked up at them without envy. He would have raised a glass if he'd had one but it was too early in the day for that, the streets still chilled and the burnt diesel of the double-deckers sharp in his nostrils. They had found mammoth bones here, he remembered, when they were digging the first underground in the 1860s. He lifted his leg to step over a monstrous tibia. An archaeopteryx flapped like a garish broken parasol from the tower of St Mary's blotting out the clock-face. He scurried through the arch into the courtyard of Queen's, raising a hand to the outside porter.

Evaluation: Duffy's vision of London offers us a choice between two futures – 'Hierusalem the Golden' or Hell. Her novel involves the reader in the outcome of this choice and makes us aware of our responsibility in learning the lessons of the past. In this sense, the novel is much more than simply an historical panorama, taking on a political dimension. Written in 1975 and depicting the changing landscape of the city as old communities are broken up and property redeveloped, *Capital* is as alive to the present as it is to the past, and in its foreboding sense of a city under threat it anticipates the role of Thatcherism in accelerating the growing inequalities she describes. In this light, *Capital* can be seen as a pioneering book and one that points the way to the more overtly political novels of the 1980s and beyond.

The London Revival

'At its best London fiction has, in the past twenty years, become characteristically a visionary medium.'

Michael Moorcock, Introduction to
Lud Heat and Suicide Bridge, Iain Sinclair (1995)

In recent years it is fair to say that London writing has enjoyed a noticeable revival of fortune. The city itself has undergone a dramatic transformation since the Thatcherite-driven changes of the 1980s and much London writing has been produced in response to this perceived challenge to the city's identity. Novels such as Michael Moorcock's *Mother London* (1988) and Iain Sinclair's *Downriver* (1991) both characterise the 1980s as marking a break with the past and demonise Thatcher as the mother of all London's recent misfortunes. But through the nineties and a change in the political landscape the stream of London novels has shown little sign of abating. The reasons for this may be bound up with the rebranding of the city as part of 'Cool Britannia' and the specific marketing of novels as London-based. Ironically, it has been those areas of the city most affected by regeneration in the 1980s that are now the focus of renewed interest into London's past.

It seems to me that this plethora of new writing can be largely divided into two separate streams. In the first are those novels that are primarily character-driven and whose characters are symbolic of the city they inhabit, such as Martin Amis' *Money* (1984) and *London Fields* (1989), or extend interpersonal and family relationships to comment on the state of the city as a whole, such as Zadie Smith's *White Teeth* (2000) and Monica Ali's *Brick Lane* (2003). These novels, along with others such as Hanif Kureishi's *The Buddha of Suburbia* (1990) and Nick Hornby's tales of North London lives in *High Fidelity* (1995) and *About a Boy* (1998), do not tackle the representation of London directly but use the city as a backdrop and might at a time when London writing is less fashionable be classified quite differently.

To my mind, more interesting and more committed examples of London writing can be found in the second stream of novels, those that examine the influence of the city on the behaviour of its inhabitants. Such novels explore the changing layout of the city and may be loosely termed as topographical, for example JG Ballard's trilogy of novels from the 1970s, *Crash* (1973), *Concrete Island* (1974) and *High-Rise* (1975), all of which explore the extremes to which human behaviour may be provoked by the built environment. These novels explore the outer limits of the city, but have been extremely influential on novelists such as Michael Moorcock, Iain Sinclair and others such as Chris Petit, whose novel *Robinson* (1991) has been described as a Ballardian exploration of the inner city.

Stewart Home's *Red London* (1994), Geoff

Nicholson's *Bleeding London* (1997) and Nicholas Royle's *The Director's Cut* (2000) all demonstrate an explicit awareness of London as a site of topographical investigation and place the city at the heart of these novels. This emphasis on place has increasingly been combined with an attempt to mine the vertical seam of the city's history and here Iain Sinclair and Peter Ackroyd may be identified as the chief exponents of fictional forays into London's past, but having already discussed these writers in connection with their use of occult themes I will turn my attention here to other figures. Moorcock, Petit and Royle represent what is for me the true tradition of London writing and they are joined by Angela Carter, whose novel *Wise Children* (1991) is a marvellously theatrical account of London's recent history. Finally, Martin Amis' *London Fields* (1989) gains entry here chiefly because it seems impossible to ignore. One of the most iconic books of the 1980s and the winner of a *Time Out* readers' poll of London writing, Amis' sophisticated comic novel has little in common with the other writers discussed here, or, it might seem, with the city from which it derives its title. Its inclusion here is less an acknowledgement of its popularity as a London novel than a concession to its undoubted influence on other London writers such as Will Self and Geoff Dyer.

Michael Moorcock, *Mother London* (1988)

Author and Background: Michael Moorcock was born in London in 1939 and began writing in his teens. He has since produced an enormous number of novels and short stories, mainly in the genres of science fiction and epic fantasy. From 1964 to 1971 he was the editor of the influential avant-garde magazine *New Worlds*, in which he published much of JG Ballard's early experimental fiction. Moorcock remains most closely associated with the counter-culture of the sixties through his character Jerry Cornelius, who appears in a sequence of novels culminating in *The Condition of Muzak* (1977), which won the Guardian Fiction Prize. Perhaps as a result of his remarkable fluency and the perennially unfashionable status of fantasy fiction, his reputation has suffered and Moorcock remains one of our most neglected novelists.

Mother London (1988) was the first of Moorcock's books to take London as its subject matter and it was followed by a sequel, *King of the City* (2000), as well as by a collection of London-themed short stories, *London Bone* (2001). These books have been something of a departure for Moorcock, although they are written in his familiarly dense and exuberantly inventive style. Yet beneath the celebratory tone and elegiac depiction of the London of Moorcock's youth, *Mother London* is also a political novel that challenges the Thatcherite assault that has resulted in the destruction of many of the landscapes recorded here.

Plot Summary: A sprawling epic and a Dickensian attempt to capture the city in its entirety, *Mother London* has a complex structure that alternately moves toward and withdraws from its chronological centre – the Blitz of 1940. Around this central moment, the novel records the history of the city through the intervening years as experienced by the novel's three major characters. These are David Mummery, a writer and detached observer of the city, Joseph Kiss, an actor and occasional tour-guide whose knowledge of London is equally vast and Mary Gasalee, who awakens from a coma to become the lover of both these men and ultimately the wife of Joseph Kiss.

These three characters are described as the 'Celebrants' and it is through their interwoven personal histories that Moorcock establishes his portrait of the city. We witness the trauma of the Blitz that leaves Mary Gasalee in a coma and provides Joseph Kiss with his moment of heroism, the immigration and resultant prejudice of the 1950s, the emerging counter-culture of the 1960s and finally the political changes of the 1970s and 80s. Through the years these characters are united by their telepathic ability to hear the voices of Londoners past and present, a skill that is as much a curse as a blessing and which leads to a spell in the asylum where they are first introduced. Interspersed through the narrative are these intrusive voices which act as a commentary on the unfolding events and which supply an overview of the prevailing attitudes of the city's inhabitants. From every corner of the city, *Mother London* records half a century of London's history through the perspective of those lost voices left unheard in the official testimony to the city's past.

Key London Scene: David Mummery, an 'urban anthropologist', writes memorials to London's legendary past, a history that he views as akin to a symphony and whose music may be heard by those attuned to the voices of the past:

> Momentarily Mummery feels as if London's population has been transformed into music, so sublime is his vision; the city's inhabitants create an exquisitely complex geometry, a geography passing beyond the natural to become metaphysical, only describable in terms of music or abstract physics; nothing else makes sense of relationships between roads, rails, waterways, subways, sewers, tunnels, bridges, viaducts, aqueducts, cables, between every kind of intersection. Mummery hums a tune of his own improvising and up they come still, his Londoners, like premature daisies, sometimes singing, or growling, or whistling, chattering; each adding a further harmony or motif to this miraculous spontaneity, up into the real world.

Evaluation: Mother London reads more as a memorial to the past than it does a celebration of the present. The Blitz is presented as London's finest hour, a mythical moment now passed and never to be repeated, for London's post-war history has been something of an opportunity lost, a time when the necessary reforms that the city's rebuilding might have facilitated were thwarted by compromise and a lack of vision. Alongside the affectionate recall of days gone by, Moorcock's novel displays a real anger at what he perceives to be an all too avoidable decline.

The novel's dense and complex structure can be frustrating at times, but it avoids a linear narrative in order to emphasise London's circular history, in which events from the past are constantly replayed. In this manner, London's myths and legends are invoked once again as the wholesale changes imposed upon the city in the 1980s threaten to extinguish these voices forever.

Martin Amis, *London Fields* (1989)

Author and Background: Martin Amis was born in Oxford in 1949 and studied English at Oxford University. His first novel, *The Rachael Papers*, was published in 1974 and was later filmed. He has since written a further nine novels, including *Money* (1984), *London Fields* (1989), *The Information* (1993) and most recently *Yellow Dog* (2004). In addition, he has produced several volumes of short stories and criticism, as well as an autobiography, *Experience* (2000).

London Fields was recently voted Londoners' favourite London novel in a *Time Out* readers' poll, but the London that features here and in his earlier novel *Money* is by no means the faithful approximation of reality to be found in many other London novels. For Amis' London is a grotesque caricature of the city, a monstrous comic creation characterised by the hellish blend of greed and fear that animate his equally repellent cast of Londoners. London is no more than a fictional backdrop for these bleakly drawn satires and these novels often appear only to diminish the city, repeatedly representing London as a cheap and inferior imitation of its American counterparts. *London Fields* does not portray its Hackney namesake and instead revels in its depiction of the nightmarish boozers and rubbish-strewn streets of Ladbroke Grove, but beneath this sophisticated parody of West London life there is little evidence of an abiding affection for the city.

Plot Summary: London Fields has three characters at its heart: Keith Talent, a lowlife thug, criminal and darts fanatic; Nicola Six, an unattainably beautiful and manipulative woman following a mysterious agenda; and Guy Clinch, a conventional and wealthy man with an ambitious wife and overactive infant. Meeting in the unlikely venue of the Black Cross, a disreputable and downmarket boozer, these are three characters in search of a murderer. For the novel is a murder mystery in reverse, in which it is the murder itself towards which the narrative unfolds. Keith is the obvious candidate for murderer, Nicola as victim and Guy as fall guy, but as the story unfolds these roles become less clear as Nicola skilfully manipulates her two would-be lovers, playing them off against each other and destroying their lives in the process. As we track their plans and schemes against the backdrop of a decaying city, it becomes clear that this relationship is not a threesome but a foursome, for the novel's narrator, increasingly unwilling to be merely a detached observer, begins to take an active role in the story he is narrating. As the novel closes with Guy's marriage in ruins and Keith's dreams of becoming a darts celebrity in tatters, it is neither of them but instead the narrator himself who steps into the story in the final pages to commit the long-awaited murder of Nicola Six.

Key London Scene: The Black Cross pub is the spiritual home of *London Fields'* hero, the dart-wielding, beer-swilling Keith Talent, and as such it symbolises the entire seedy world of lowlife London:

TV AND DARTS, said the sign. AND PINBALL. The first time Guy entered the Black Cross he was a man pushing through the black door of his fear... He survived. He lived. The place was ruined and innocuous in its northern light: a clutch of dudes and Rastas playing pool over the damp swipe of the baize, the pewtery sickliness of the whites (they looked like war footage), the twittering fruit-machines, the fuming pie-warmer. Guy asked for a drink in the only voice he had; he didn't tousle his hair or his accent; he carried no tabloid under his arm, open on the racing page. With a glass of medium-sweet white wine he moved to the pinball table, an old Gottlieb, with Arabian-Nights artwork (temptress, devil, hero, maiden) – Eye of the Tiger. Eye of the Tiger... A decrepit Irish youth stood inches away whispering who's the boss who's the boss into Guy's ear for as long as he seemed to need to do that. Whenever Guy looked up a dreadful veteran of the pub, his face twanging in the canned rock, stared at him bitterly, like the old man you stop for at the zebra who crosses slowly, with undiminished suspicion: no forgiveness there, not ever.

Evaluation: London Fields is many things – a murder mystery, a kind of love story, a postmodern experiment in form – but is it primarily a London novel? For the London Amis has created here often appears to be little more than the imaginary space necessary to support the existence of a character such as Keith Talent. Ultimately it is his London, not ours, and *London Fields* must be judged on its comic skill and verbal inventiveness rather than upon its portrayal of the city. In his foreword to the novel Amis acknowledges his difficulty in choosing the title of the book and one suspects that under a different name this book would not have come to be regarded as a London novel at all.

Angela Carter, *Wise Children* (1991)

Author and Background: Angela Carter was born in 1940 and attended Bristol University. She spent many years in Japan, Australia and the USA, but much of her fiction returns to her home in South London. Her first novel, *Shadow Dance*, was published in 1965. This was followed by *The Magic Toyshop* (1967), *Heroes and Villains* (1969), *Love* (1971), *The Passion of New Eve* (1977) and *Nights at the Circus* (1984), as well as by several volumes of short stories and collected journalism. She died in 1992.

The Magic Toyshop tells the tale of a country girl who comes to live with her relations in Brixton, while *Nights at the Circus* recreates the theatrical world of the Victorian city, but it is in her last novel, *Wise Children* (1991), that we find her most sustained work of London fiction. With its fantastical sense of the past, this novel creates a cast of exuberant and larger than life characters reminiscent of Michael Moorcock's *Mother London* and as the complex family histories are unravelled we witness the changing fortunes of the city that supports them.

Plot Summary: Wise Children is a novel that relates the tangled histories of two theatrical families, the Hazards and the Chances, alongside a supporting cast of assorted family members whose often uncertain parentage provides much of the comic impetus. Against a backdrop of music hall, theatre and film, the now aged Chance sisters, Nora and Dora, look back over their long and eventful lives in showbusiness from the Brixton home where they were born. The Chances are from South London, very much the wrong side of the tracks, and their struggles are at odds with the privileged lives of the established Shakespearian actors of the Hazard dynasty.

The novel begins with the twins receiving an invitation to their (unacknowledged) father, Sir Melchior Hazard's one-hundredth birthday party, an event with which the novel closes. In-between we follow the lives of Nora and Dora through a series of triumphs and disasters as they move from London to Hollywood and back in pursuit of their careers and a series of increasingly unlikely and unsuitable lovers. These adventures are related with a theatrical flourish and culminate in a fantastic party in which the book's cast are reunited for one final performance as family secrets are aired, children are finally acknowledged by their parents and Nora and Dora steal the show.

Key London Scene: Looking from the window of the Brixton home they have inhabited for almost a century, the Chance sisters watch as the familiar London of their youth is gradually replaced with something more alien to them:

You can see for miles, out of this window. You can see right across the river. There's Westminster Abbey, see? Flying the St George's cross today. St. Paul's, the single breast. Big Ben, winking in its golden eye. Not much else familiar, these days. This is about the time that comes in every century when they reach out for all that they can grab of dear old London, and pull it down. Then they build it up again, like London Bridge in the nursery rhyme, goodbye, hello, but it's never the same. Even the railway stations, changed out of recognition, turned into souks. Waterloo. Victoria. Nowhere you can get a decent cup of tea, all they give you is Harvey Wallbangers, filthy cappuccino. Stocking shops and knicker outlets everywhere you look. I said to Nora; 'Remember *Brief Encounter*, how I cried buckets? Nowhere for them to meet on a station, nowadays, except in a bloody knicker shop. Their hands would have to shyly touch under a cover of a pair of Union Jack boxer shorts.

Evaluation: Wise Children opens with a question, 'Why is London like Budapest? A. Because it is two cities divided by a river.' And the London that Carter recreates here is one in which the old divisions of north and south, rich and poor, are as evident today as they ever were. Carter's baroque prose can be something of an acquired taste and while it has been described as magic realism, at times the book reads less as a novel than as a riotous pantomime that provides an amusing spectacle but which is difficult to take seriously. But ultimately Carter's inventiveness and wit are hard to resist and like a skilled theatrical performer she maintains complete control of her cast throughout.

Christopher Petit, *Robinson* (1993)

Author and Background: Chris Petit was born in 1949 and educated in Yorkshire and at Bristol University. After arriving in London, he became film editor for *Time Out* magazine, where he worked from 1973–8, and his first film, *Radio On* (1979), was co-produced by Wim Wenders. He has made several further films, including *An Unsuitable Job for a Woman* (1981) and *Chinese Boxes* (1984), as well as television essays in conjunction with JG Ballard and Iain Sinclair. *Robinson* (1993) was Petit's first book and was followed by a further London novel, *The Hard Shoulder*, in 2001. He has in addition written a number of thrillers, including *The Psalm Killer*, *Back From the Dead* and *The Human Pool*.

Robinson has been described as 'the most implicated successor to the *Crash* template', and is clearly influenced by Ballard's series of apocalyptic London novels incorporating the now familiar imagery of urban breakdown, sex and violence, but in this case transporting the action from the suburbs to the centre. But the book is equally allied to Patrick Keiller's film *London* (1993), whose central character is also named Robinson and who provides a similarly ironic commentary of a declining city. Alive to the tradition of London writing that preceded it, *Robinson* provides a further reminder of its origins through the character Cookie, loosely based on that purveyor of London *noir*, Robin Cook, aka Derek Raymond.

Plot Summary: The nameless narrator meets Robinson for the first time in Soho, where, aside from a few brief road trips, the novel is set. Robinson is both strangely familiar and mysteriously enigmatic – he appears to know everybody yet nobody knows him, and, fuelled by a constant stream of drink and drugs, he moves from pub to pub following a series of strange obsessions. Soon the narrator has abandoned his own life for Robinson's world, where he becomes involved in a twilight existence of parties and night-time drives across the city. The narrator finds himself working in Robinson's bookshop and living in a shared house with an old-school spiv and fixer called Cookie. Gradually the relationship between these two characters and Robinson himself becomes increasingly strained, as Robinson embarks on a new venture as the director of porn movies. A combination of drink, drugs and sex is compounded by Robinson's increasingly erratic and violent behaviour, which ultimately leads to the death of Cookie, killed as Robinson films. This mental disintegration is mirrored in the decline of the city itself and as the novel closes in a hallucinatory scene, London is flooded by endless rain.

Key London Scene: As the narrator's perception of reality becomes increasingly blurred, so the city itself becomes indistinguishable from the films that are shot there, London becoming a bizarre collage waiting to be filmed:

Other images came instead. Many of them I cut into Robinson's film. I saw a woman swinging out her right arm. William Blake walking down Poland Street, shadowed by a dog. The gunmen waiting on the grassy knoll. I saw the doors in my life (save those with her). Blind Borges wrote: I saw a tattered labyrinth (it was London). I saw myself as a child standing at a window and the shadow of my mother, her voice saying, 'Come away now'; Cookie and the sly look of the wild, feral girl. A moving walkway at Gatwick airport; tank manoeuvres in the desert. I saw the children I never had; Marlene Dietrich telling Orson Welles, 'Your future's all used up.' Traffic lights changing in empty streets. Lee Marvin walking through LAX, his footsteps like gunshots. I watched a game show host position his guests on the camera mark. A Texaco station on a road out of Felixstowe, overhead a jet plane on its penultimate flight before crashing… I saw a photograph of Rainer Werner Fassbinder directing Veronica Ross, watched George Best send a goalkeeper the wrong way. In the wake of a power cruiser, children run on

Hampstead Heath. Test crash footage of wired-up dummies in cars. Brendan Behan drunk and roaring, 'At least I don't fuck my own dogs.' The wall against which the Ceaușescus were shot. Weeds on a building site; the rolling credits of a TV comedy (the last one); the slap of the Thames against London Bridge…

Evaluation: Robinson reads as a composite of other London novels, a single text comprising an entire tradition in which images are superimposed upon one another, sparking bizarre new connections. This is a team effort combining Ballard's midnight drives through an abandoned city, as well as his apocalyptic visions of a drowned London, Iain Sinclair's accounts of books and bookdealers, the seedy Soho world of Gerald Kersh, the casual violence of Derek Raymond. The whole thing is bound together with Petit's filmmaker's eye, making *Robinson* both a curious one-off and a homage to London as a fictional setting.

Nicholas Royle, *The Director's Cut* (2000)

Author and Background: Born in Sale, Cheshire, in 1963, Nicholas Royle is the author of five novels: *Counterparts* (1993), *Saxophone Dreams* (1996), *The Matter of the Heart* (1997), *The Director's Cut* (2000) and most recently *Antwerp* (2004). He has also produced more than 100 short stories and edited several anthologies. Having lived in West London for many years he now lives in Manchester.

Of his novels, the two books dealing most closely with London are *The Matter of the Heart* and *The Director's Cut*. The former has been described as 'Iain Sinclair psycho-geographic incantation meets Jeremy Clarkson auto-porn on the Australian highway' and explores the way locations may resonate with the memories of earlier events, in this case linking a nine-teenth-century attempt at heart-transplant surgery with a now abandoned hospital. This interest in abandoned spaces is something of an obsession for Royle and forms a major part of *The Director's Cut*, a novel that also displays his knowledge of London film and film loca-tions (both Chris Petit's *Radio On* and Patrick Keiller's *London* are name-checked here). This focus upon the crossover between film and text and the apprehension of the city as a film set is characteristic of many current London writers from Royle and Petit to Sinclair and Ballard, as well as earlier writers in a similar tradition such as Graham Greene.

Plot Summary: On a demolition site off the Tottenham Court Road a body is found wrapped in rolls of film. The victim is Iain Burns, who died 15 years before in an apparent suicide and whose death was filmed by four aspiring young directors. These four have since had largely disappointing careers as their early obsessions and hopes have been compromised and all of their lives have been transformed by this death. Harry Foxx, a frustrated art house director, Frank, a womaniser and film critic haunted by the death of his wife Sarah, Richard Charnock, who has sacrificed critical acclaim for commercial success, and oddball Angelo obsessed by London's old cinemas.

The discovery of Burns' body forces these characters to come to terms with their pasts, but also to question exactly what happened on the night of Burns' death. Gradually it becomes apparent that Burns' death, along with the death of Frank's wife, as well as the series of Hammersmith Tube Murders, may all be connected and that one of them is the killer. The novel explores the obsessive interest in London's lost and abandoned spaces that haunts these characters and gradually we learn that one of these men is not who he seems. As the novel closes the narrative criss-crosses the city, finally reaching an abandoned railway depot where the killer is unmasked and where he meets his death.

Key London Scene: In *The Director's Cut* London is defined more by its existence on film than it is as an actual place. It is a city of film locations and its cinemas are the sites through which the city may be mapped:

The Screen on the Green grips and perplexes its audience with one man's obsessive imposition of patterns on to the landscape in *The Draughtsman's Contract*. Rainer Maria Fassbinder holds court at the Everyman with Lili Marleen and *The Marriage of Eva Braun*. West to the Classic, where *ET* teases out tears from hardened Kilburnites; floating high above the flickering ribbons of the Westway and a fan of railway tracks heading out of Paddington, each train a strip of celluloid with its lighted window frames and silhouetted actors; then down to the Electric with Wim Wenders' *Hammett* proving a puzzle to the trustafarians of Notting Hill. South now, over the Coronet and the Gate to Drayton Gardens, where the Paris Pullman is on its own last reel, set to close within months. Against even the glittering head-lamps of several thousand taxi cabs and the burning ruby light clusters of a million private cars, the cinemas of London are its beacons – even when they're dark.

Evaluation: The Director's Cut is a novel that explores the obsessions that the city can arouse. With its series of abandoned buildings and closed cinemas, its depiction of underground journeys and empty railway sidings, the novel carefully maps and reshapes the city through the eyes of its protagonists, exploring the unexpected and sinister ways in which they all attempt to bring order to the chaos that surrounds them. Using an apparently straightforward thriller format, the novel cleverly subverts our expectations by creating an otherworldly city in which everybody has the freedom to devise an identity of their own choosing and to follow their own obsessions regardless of where they might lead.

The Thirty Essential London Novels

In order of publication:

Charles Dickens, *Bleak House* (1853)

Richard Jefferies, *After London* (1885)

Robert Louis Stevenson, *The Strange Case of Dr Jekyll and Mr Hyde* (1886)

Sir Arthur Conan Doyle, *A Study in Scarlet* (1887)

William Morris, *News From Nowhere* (1890)

George Gissing, *New Grub Street* (1891)

Arthur Machen, *The Great God Pan* (1894)

HG Wells, *The War of the Worlds* (1898)

Joseph Conrad, *The Secret Agent* (1907)

Virginia Woolf, *Mrs Dalloway* (1925)

Evelyn Waugh, *Vile Bodies* (1930)

Gerald Kersh, *Night and the City* (1938)

Patrick Hamilton, *Hangover Square* (1941)

Henry Green, *Caught* (1943)

Elizabeth Bowen, *The Heat of the Day* (1948)

Margery Allingham, *The Tiger in the Smoke* (1952)

Samuel Selvon, *The Lonely Londoners* (1956)

JG Ballard, *The Drowned World* (1962)

Alexander Baron, *The Lowlife* (1963)

Maureen Duffy, *Capital* (1975)

LONDON WRITING

Peter Ackroyd, *Hawksmoor* (1985)
Iain Sinclair, *White Chappell Scarlet Tracings* (1987)
Michael Moorcock, *Mother London* (1988)
Martin Amis, *London Fields* (1989)
Derek Raymond, *I Was Dora Suarez* (1990)
Angela Carter, *Wise Children* (1991)
Christopher Petit, *Robinson* (1993)
Neil Gaiman, *Neverwhere* (1996)
Anthony Frewin, *London Blues* (1997)
Nicholas Royle, *The Director's Cut* (2000)

Further Reading

London writing is as voluminous as the city it describes and the books listed here barely scratch the surface. These titles do, however, provide a representative overview of both the writers and the themes that I have explored in this book, as well as directing the reader towards the wider historical and cultural background:

Ackroyd, Peter (ed), Sir Arthur Conan Doyle, *The Sign of Four*, London: Penguin, 2001

London: The Biography, London: Chatto & Windus, 2000

The Collection, London: Chatto & Windus, 2001

Allen, Rick, *The Moving Pageant: A Literary Sourcebook on London Street Life 1700–1914,* London: Routledge, 1998

Bailey, Paul (ed), *The Oxford Book of London*, Oxford: OUP, 1995

Carter, Angela, *Expletives Deleted*, London: Chatto & Windus, 1992

Cavaliero, Glenn, *The Supernatural and English Fiction*, Oxford: OUP, 1995

Cunningham, Ian, *A Reader's Guide to Writer's London*, London: Prion Books, 2001

Duncan, Andrew, *Secret London*, London: New Holland, 1995

Gilbert, Pamela K (ed), *Imagined Londons*, New York: State University of New York, 2002

Glinert, Ed, *The London Compendium*, London: Allen Lane, 2003

Greenland, Colin, *Michael Moorcock: Death Is No Obstacle*, Manchester: Savoy Books, 1992

Home, Stewart, *The Assault on Culture*, Edinburgh: AK Press, 1991

Humphreys, Rob, *London: The Rough Guide*, London: Rough Guides, 2003

Jabubowski, Maxim (ed), *London Noir*, London: Serpent's Tail, 1994

Jack, Ian (ed), *Granta 65: The Lives of the City*, London: Granta, Spring 1999

Keiller, Patrick *Robinson in Space*, London: Reaktion, 1999

Kerr, Joe & Gibson, Andrew (eds), *London – From Punk to Blair*, London: Reaktion, 2003

Lachman, Gary, *The Dedalus Book of the Occult*, Cambridge: Dedalus, 2003

Lehan, Richard, *The City in Literature: An Intellectual and Cultural History*, Berkeley: University of California, 1998

Lexton, Maria (ed), *Time Out Book of London Short Stories*, London: Penguin, 1993

Lichtenstein, Rachael and Sinclair, Iain, *Rodinsky's Room*, London: Granta, 1999

Litvinoff, Emanuel, *Journey Through a Small Planet* London: Michael Joseph, 1972

Luckhurst, Roger, *The Angle Between Two Walls – The Fiction of JG Ballard*, Liverpool: Liverpool University Press, 1997

Machen, Arthur, *The London Adventure, or The Art of Wandering*, London: Martin Secker, 1924

Madox Ford, Ford, *The Soul of London*, London: Alston Rivers, 1905

Mighall, Robert (ed), Robert Louis Stevenson, *The Strange Case of Dr Jekyll and Mr Hyde and Other Tales of Terror*, London: Penguin, 2002

Palmer, Alan, *The East End: Four Centuries of London Life*, London: John Murray, 1989

Parrinder, Patrick, '"These fragments I have shored against my ruins": Visions of a Ruined London from Edmund Spenser to JG Ballard', in Onega & Stotesbury (eds), *London in Literature: Visionary Mappings of the Metropolis*, Heidelberg: University of Heidelberg Press, 2002

Phillips, Mike, *London Crossings: A Biography of Black Britain*, London: Continuum, 2002

Platt, Edward, *Leadville: A Biography of the A40*, London: Picador, 2000

Porter, Roy, *London: A Social History*, London: Hamish Hamilton, 1994

Quindlen, Anna, *Imagined London*, Washington: National Geographic Society, 2004

Raban, Jonathan, *Soft City*, London: Hamish Hamilton, 1974

Rennison, Nick (ed), *Waterstone's Guide to London Writing*, London: Waterstone's Booksellers Ltd, 1999

Rogerson, Barnaby (ed), *Poetry of Place: London*, London: Baring & Rogerson, 2003

Royle, Nicholas (ed), *Time Out Book of London Stories Volume 2*, London: Penguin, 2000

Sinclair, Iain (ed), Alexander Baron, *The Lowlife*, London: Harvill, 2001

(ed) Sir Arthur Conan Doyle, *A Study in Scarlet*, London: Penguin, 2001

Crash, London: BFI, 1999

Lights Out for the Territory, London: Granta, 1997

London Orbital, London: Granta, 2002

Lud Heat and Suicide Bridge, London: Granta, 1998

Smith, Stephen, *Underground London,* London: Abacus 2004

Sorensen, Colin, *London on Film: 100 Years of Film Making in London,* London: Museum of London, 1996

Symons, Julian, *Bloody Murder – The Detective Story to the Crime Novel: A History,* London: Faber, 1972

Trench, Richard and Hillman, Ellis, *London Under London,* London: John Murray, 1984

Vallance, Rosalind (ed), *Dickens' London,* London: Folio Society, 1966

Weightman, Gavin & Humphries, Steve, *The Making of Modern London 1815–1914,* London: Sidgwick & Jackson, 1983

Weinreb, Ben and Hibbert, Christopher, *The London Encyclopaedia,* London: Macmillan, 1983

Wilson, AN (ed), *The Faber Book of London,* London: Faber, 1993

Wolfreys, Julian, *Writing London: The Trace of the Urban Text from Blake to Dickens,* London: Palgrave Macmillan, 1998

Writing London: Materiality, Memory, Spectrality, London: Palgrave Macmillan, 2004

Woodcock, Peter, *This Enchanted Isle – The Neo-Romantic Vision from William Blake to the New Visionaries,* Glastonbury: Gothic Image, 2000

Wright, Patrick, *A Journey Through Ruins – The Last Days of London,* London: Radius, 1991

Zarate, Oscar (ed), *It's Dark in London,* London: Serpent's Tail, 1996

Index

159

INDEX